THE

NARROWROAD

A Guide to Legacy Wealth

Dr. Pamela C.V. Jolly

where words connect

THE

NARROWROAD

A Guide to Legacy Wealth

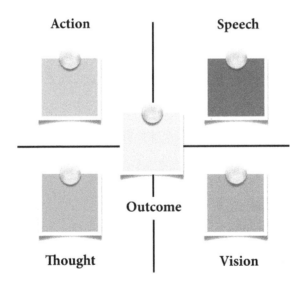

Dr. Pamela C.V. Jolly

ISBN: 978-1-946274-78-6 (Hardcover)
ISBN: 978-1-946274-79-3 (e-Book)
Library of Congress Control Number : 2022931870

Cover Design: Omomota
Graphic Design: Dr. Pamela Jolly
Layout: Amit Dey

Second Edition Published by Wordeee in the United States, Beacon, New York 2022
Register your book at https://PJolly.com/register

Website: www.wordeee.com
Twitter: twitter.com/wordeee
Facebook: Facebook.com/wordeee
e-mail: contact@wordeee.com

Printed in the USA

TABLE OF CONTENTS

Praise for The NarrowRoad vii

Dedication xii

Foreword xiii

Author's Journey xv

PART 1 . . . . **xxvi**

The NarrowRoad Overview 1

PART 2 . . . . **17**

1. Our History 18

2. Entering The NarrowRoad: Key Requirements Along
   The NarrowRoad 28

3. Rules of the Road: 62

4. Portfolio of Talents 70

5. Capital Along The NarrowRoad: The Business of You.. 76

6. Understanding Capital Relationship and its Influence Over
   Degrees of Freedom 96

7. The Terrains in the Wilderness 112

8. Weathering the Storm: The Power of Collaboration 132

9. Understanding the Financial Wilderness 141

10. Life, Liberty, and the Pursuit 149

11. The Legacy Thread 163

12. Wealth Creation 171

13. Journeying Beyond The NarrowRoad...to Emancipation . . . 194

14. Legacy Wealth at Last: Reviewing Lessons Learned on
    The NarrowRoad—It will Work if You Work It 210

15. Why We Can't Wait. 226

Glossary of Terms 236

Appendix 240

Acknowledgments. 242

PRAISE FOR THE NARROWROAD

A must-read. Dr. Pamela Jolly lays out a masterful journey of self-discovery, providing historical and biblical context while leading us through the perfect framework to achieve legacy wealth. This book is compelling, logical, culturally relevant, and exactly what I needed to ignite my flame to take action towards my goals. I highly recommend this book to all those looking to create, grow, build and expand wealth their way. The concepts around The Narrow-Road Identity are a game changer! Dr. Jolly cracks the code and gives us the tools to overcome our blind spots and lean into our hidden talents. After reading this book, I've taken a more aggressive stance toward my financial goals and estate planning, and I'm well on my way to becoming a successful WEALTH-BUILDER. Bravo, Dr. Jolly, well done!

—Avis Scott
Vice President Merchandising Retail Home Furnishing

Excellent guide. Wish I had access to this book in my early 20s as a primer for adulthood. This is a transforming book that will help you change your mindset toward wealth. A great resource for all generations. Very resourceful and practical guide to making the right choices as I think ahead for my future goals.

—Dr. Hansie Mathlier
Cardiologist, Philadelphia

If you are seeking information on how you can leave a legacy, then you must read The NarrowRoad, written by Dr. Pamela C. Jolly. It's innovative, creative and it ensures sound leadership to follow when seeking to leave a legacy. It presents a world of endless possibilities.

— **Lois R. Blackshear**
Retired mathematician

The second edition of the book by Pamela C. Jolly, the founder and CEO of Torch enterprise Inc., is a blessing. I, Rev. Jeannette Thomas Shegog, was blessed to take her first class in The NarrowRoad, a Guide to Legacy Wealth. She introduced our family to the definition of legacies that our parents and grandparents had given the Thomas family and how it should be used. Pamela is an optimistic, loving, passionate and positive person in teaching us the meaning of how to effectively use our remaining property. She has an amazing power to build confidence that ALL PEOPLE can and should build this legacy together. She gave us all the tools and all the methods we needed to move mountains. We can now rise and meet our potential. This is the best course I have taken. It is an excellent book!

Absolutely transformative! After decades of trying to mobilize our extended family to leverage our family land, Dr. Jolly's book, The NarrowRoad, helped focus three generations to work collaboratively in building a plan to achieve our goals of collective wealth. Our legacy thanks you!!

—**Rev. Jeannette Thomas Shegog**

What I love most about The NarrowRoad journey is the feeling of agency. Achieving generational wealth together is possible – and Dr. Jolly's strategic guidance and blueprint ensured that the three generations of my family could dream and build wealth our way. Our legacy thanks you!

I appreciated the comprehensive approach to defining wealth in Dr. Jolly's The NarrowRoad, considering social capital, intellectual capital, spiritual capital, and financial capital. With this expanded vision, Dr. Jolly ensures that everyone can contribute to building wealth and no one is left behind.

—**Beverly Watson**
Business Executive

The NarrowRoad is a process that helped bring our family together; seamlessly tie a rich African-American history and work through past trauma in order to establish the foundation for creating personal and family generational wealth plans and actions.

—**Dr. Marya Shegog**
Health Equity and Diversity Coordinator

Thank you so much for taking on this journey with me. It definitely was uncharted territory. I greatly appreciate your council. I am making more money than I've ever made before. I work at a college, and I have two kids in college, and it's free! I have invited others in, instead of believing the lie that I am always on my own. I will definitely be looking at other multiple streams of income and bringing those to fruition.

—**Daphne Cook**
Cohort Member of the Omaha Legacy Wealth Initiatives

Thank you for helping me see the value of wealth and a well-rounded vision for my future. Today, despite a pandemic, no new clients, and most of my clients having to cancel their events, we have money to pay all of our bills and a reserve to last us a few months. My family also has a collective mindset of focusing on what is important, not just money. Our community needs this, and possibly now more than ever. Thank you for being a blessing, Dr. Pamela C. Jolly.

—Aisha Winfield
Entrepreneur AIB marketing and Consulting

I'm writing to say thank you for taking the time to write this book. Your advice on the pros and cons of going it alone in my wealth journey helped a lot. Teaching me to get comfortable with a better understanding of my business before rushing into investing. Thank you for empowering me with the information you provided.

—Kistein Monkhouse
Founder of Patient Orator

The NarrowRoad didn't just take courage to write but to read. There were multiple times when I stopped reading the book and had to assess where I was in my own Journey. The relationship that Dr. Jolly highlights between Kingdom work, Inheritance, Purpose and Legacy are one we all need but most aren't ready for. You can't read this book and operate the same as you did prior. I have a better understanding of who I am and what I've been called to do as a result of this work. I'm very grateful for her courage and what it cost her to write and share.

—John Matthew Borders IV
Founder Vth & Madison

I still have so many things I need and intend to implement which I learned from The NarrowRoad Women and Wealth Initiative, but I have a road map now.

I turn to the lessons learned, again and again, to ensure that I am building something which I can pass on, yes, but also live into now as well.

I thought I was too old to create any wealth not resourced enough to even bother trying.

Learning that I needed to take stock of what I already have and begin where I am has been a game-changer. You cannot build wealth on an impoverished mindset

When I was able to recognize the legacy of wealth that was passed on to me, to understand that I was starting from what my mother gave me and what her people gave her...what their people gave them, it changed my understanding. I come from wealth and the ways in which it has been passed on

Lost rerouted is not always legible, BUT it exists.

This shift has fundamentally changed what I have been able to create and share with my children and family members.

There is so much more to do, but I am armed

The NarrowRoad Women and Wealth will continue to be my North Star.

—Vashti DuBois
Executive Director, The Colored Girls Museum

DEDICATION

*This book is dedicated to the
Torch Bearers of my Legacy*

Jolly Family Tree

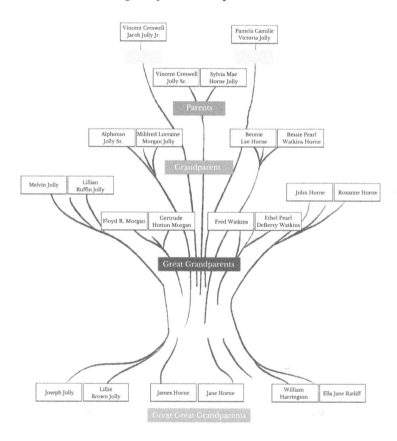

FOREWORD

I have known Pamela since high school. I've traveled down to Hampton University (my first time driving on the highway) to watch her receive her Bachelor's degree. I drove to the University of Pennsylvania's Wharton School of Business with a BBQ Chicken Pizza to help her through one of her stressful nights while earning her MBA. I was there when she returned from New Orleans after her rebuilding efforts post-Katrina, and I was there when she left for Boston University School of Theology to journey the same path Dr. Martin Luther King Jr. did to receive her doctorate. Today, I continue to travel to as many speaking engagements as possible to see her discuss legacy wealth, an idea conceived so many years ago. What I've enjoyed most about our journey and the many years I've spent with Pamela is witnessing God's answers revealed to our prayers of so many years before. Watching others in the room and seeing their light-bulb moment when they understand the premise of The NarrowRoad is always a watershed moment.

Matthew 7:13-14 is the scripture that supports the premise of The NarrowRoad. This Sermon contains the central tenets of Christian discipleship and is from the final teachings of Jesus Christ in the Sermon on the Mount. Replace the word gate with road, and you'll see this scripture puts The NarrowRoad into perspective.

Merriam-Webster has seven definitions of the word narrow. Six have negative connotations. The most fitting and at the crux of Dr. Pamela Jolly's life passion for legacy wealth is this: Narrow: careful, thorough, or minute, as a scrutiny, search, or inquiry; Road: a way or course. The NarrowRoad is just that. It is a carefully laid out process unique to each reader, connecting them to their defined promised land, legacy wealth, community, and culture.

What's in it for you (the reader)? I can only answer that by telling you what was in it for me. I have been privy to The NarrowRoad since its conception in 2004. At the time, Pamela's passion for legacy wealth creation was so far above my head. My check-to-check situation was my norm, and I thought wealth was an unattainable foreign object. Though I've heard her define capital in various ways, I was stuck on money. With my limited purview, I could only see the green paper side of capital. After hearing the concept repeatedly, I quickly realized that I was sitting on a gold mine of intellectual and social capital. It took me nine years to FINALLY see the light and turn that capital into wealth. Going through The NarrowRoad Identity, as you will too, I found out I'm a 'Doer' in the first quadrant. That means I have to do it to get it because I'm a hands-on person.

In February 2013, I became an entrepreneur. Tapping into my intellectual and social capital, I started a consulting firm. Most important to my success was that I had a guide to help me through my process. This invaluable guide offered so much more than a how-to approach. It played to my strengths and weaknesses, not only in my professional life but in my personal life as well.

My definition of wealth may not let you see me on the cover of Forbes, but I know that what I have created will leave a legacy for my child and community, thanks to Dr. Pamela C.V. Jolly, my closest friend, and her gift of The NarrowRoad.

—**Keisha L'Rae Chandler**
Senior Implementation Manager,
Professional Learning Services

AUTHOR'S JOURNEY

The Influencers of My Jolly-Journey

My cousin, Dr. Benjamin Robinson III, was the first to help me get on the road to discover my love and respect for institutional finance and banking. My father, the late Vincent Creswell Jolly, Sr., helped me narrow my road to pursue a path best suited for me to succeed. My first inflection point, over twenty-seven years ago, came during my Hampton University graduation weekend. At Denny's, over breakfast, my father would not let me leave the restaurant until I'd finished my ten-year plan. It was 1994, and he wanted me to look further down the road to 2004. He would say: "I'm proud of the steps you've taken thus far to begin a rewarding career, but it's always important to look further down the road early and make a plan to get there so as not to lose your way."

I see most things first in my mind. I'm constantly researching facts and history, looking for patterns to gain clarity around problems I see in our world and our communities. Because I "think to see," it has been the classroom that has given me the most clarity. Therefore, I've invested heavily in my ability to see through the acquisition of four degrees. Each degree heightened my awareness of the picture we all want to pose for—our purpose. Hampton University gave me an appreciation for wisdom, collaboration and a big vision. The Wharton School gave me perspective on what it means to be set apart, think bigger, and invest in what I believed. Boston University School of Theology gave me insight into the history, faith and the importance of owning one's theology. The Graduate Theological Foundation allowed me to experience various schools of thought, such as Oxford University's longstanding legacy of education and theology. In addition to all of these educational experiences, I have read thousands of books to further refine my perspective of business, finance, faith, strategy, American history, ethics, theology, women, men, purpose, and love.

My father had a saying: "the longer you are in school, the dumber you get." He used it to constantly challenge me with the question: "How are you going to translate all that education into something the average man can use?" The NarrowRoad is my attempt to deliver on his request. I want us all to understand that wealth is a right, possible and attainable with a clear vision, proven thoughts, creative actions, and authentic speech.

The CEO of NationsBank, Hugh McColl, was a great teacher in demonstrating how wealth could be created via acquisition. Within thirteen years, he had acquired more than fifty companies (including numerous banks) to create one of the largest commercial banks in the country. His ultimate desired outcome was to become the largest bank in America. I was able to see firsthand his methodology for pursuing his desired outcome during the four years I worked at NationsBank as an analyst, a commercial lender, and a vice president in treasury management.

By 2000, when I'd graduated with my MBA, I'd accomplished my Denny's ten-year plan four years early. I felt lost and unsure of my purpose. It was my mother, Sylvia Mae Horne Jolly, who then said: "You can make no mistakes if you take the time to think about your life, pray for direction, and believe—but keep it moving." It was then that I reached another inflection point and asked myself: what had I really accomplished so far; what do I still want to accomplish; what is my purpose; and where do I go from here?

At the inflection points of life, the road we travel invites us to narrow it further. We need to get very specific about what we see and don't see, and about what we desire to understand, do, and express. In taking yet another inventory of my life experiences and lessons learned thus far, I realized a few key things I'd like to share with you. My hope is that perhaps in these pages, we can both come away a little wealthier for the experience.

I have often asked myself, did my dad know I would get to the end of my first vision a decade early, only to find myself at my second inflection point ten years early, ten years post that day in Denny's? Is that why I needed to look further down the road?

On this new leg of a continuous journey, I took a leap of faith and launched my own business, Torch Enterprises, Inc. It was a radical departure from the secure world of intrapreneurship that I knew so well. The leap into the demanding and challenging world of entrepreneurship was not necessarily an easy decision, but it was a prayerful one.

To most of my peers, who aspired to be Wall Street titans, with my credentials, I was definitely taking the road less traveled. I could be making millions on the Street and be financially well-off, but I was seeking the kind of wealth that would impact generations. I was certain Torch Enterprises, Inc., was my road to take because it represented the passing of the torch from one generation to the next, the ultimate legacy play, and one far beyond financial wealth and wealth itself. Torch Enterprises was to be a firm committed to legacy. I became determined to build legacy wealth in our communities, and Torch put me squarely on a road that narrowed my choices. It forced me to devote my attention to finding answers to questions that had not yet been asked.

What I knew from my journey, thus far, was that I'd learned financial wealth early from my maternal grandmother. She stressed the importance of a savings account, having good burial insurance, a house you own, and money for the long term. I also learned that wealth was so much more than money and that wealth building is a group process. This was repeatedly confirmed when I began my career as a banker, went to business school, started my business, worked in New Orleans post-Katrina, advised more than a thousand businesses, attended seminary, and conducted research for my doctorate studies. No one does it alone. It is a group process.

Stepping Out on My "Jolly-Journey"

He that is in the shadow of wisdom is in the shadow of money, for wisdom is the cause why riches come.

—Ecclesiastes 7:12

I'm proud to be a member of the Jolly family legacy. People will often say upon meeting me and hearing me speak that I'm appropriately named. Jolly literally means to encourage someone in a lively and friendly way, and journey literally means a process of personal change and development. For the past seventeen years, the first thing that friends and family would ask me is: "Where in the world are you now?" I'd remark that I was "somewhere along the Jolly-Journey." The response stuck, and with the discovery of The NarrowRoad, I began to see that I was truly on a journey where my legacy was leading me to do what I was designed to do. My desire was to include others in the journey along The NarrowRoad to legacy wealth—let me tell you a bit about my Jolly-Journey.

I'd been raised in a home where faith, finance, legacy, wealth, and respect for generational wisdom were important.

Finding my purpose and my way to contribute to our legacy became my main focus early on in life. My father, a computer engineer, and my mother, an oncology nurse, raised me in a middle-class home with rules and structure that I abided by and grew to appreciate. Once I chose to pursue a life of purpose, the steps of my life formed a NarrowRoad. That choice placed me in dark, unfamiliar places, desperately trying to catch a glimpse of light. The first glimpse of light was a question: Where do I go from here?

I left my structured job in 2004. It had been my fourth since graduating from The Wharton School of Business in 2000. I was beginning to feel like the proverbial square peg in a round hole that I'd been called all my life. What I'd learned at Wharton, however, was that square pegs are outliers. Outliers, in statistics, are distant observation points from the more obvious ones, yet regardless of distance, they are important just the same. The world of conformity is not for outliers. We often make a way when there is no road forward.

My goal was to have a clear definition of the meaning of wealth. At the beginning of the journey, I asked myself, "Is it realistic to expect a melting pot of people with different relationships to values and money, and different levels of belief and faith to all define wealth the same way?" My answer then and now is: I don't think so. The idea of creating a pathway for individuals to define wealth on their terms became the key driver that unlocked a big part of what I call my Jolly-Journey.

Wealth is a well-balanced portfolio of assets that includes human, intellectual, social, cultural, and spiritual capital. Capital is a tool to support the building, growth, and expansion of wealth-related activities. Pooled capital can expedite the process considerably and lead to legacy wealth. After ten years on the Jolly-Journey, while synthesizing my observations and data, I finally discovered the definition of legacy wealth. It is unique to each of us and can be translated through what I termed our NarrowRoad Identity (NRID).

From a cross-section of my experiences and my academic training, I created The NarrowRoad. This unique system integrates theology, finance, business, and unblinded faith into a custom-tailored, curricula-driven pathway to wealth building. My professional and academic training allowed me to integrate varying perspectives and to coalesce the information I was learning. My research with pastors, other religious leaders and studying American history, led me to see how the Promised Land, as a concept, is indeed a sacred text that could become a unifying purpose to pursue. Regardless of faith, ethnicity and traditions, groups can organize around The NarrowRoad to pursue a path towards their inherited promise

The NarrowRoad is a system, a roadmap to help anyone discover the unique thought processes that govern their lives. For example, I'm best able to process things through observations. As a result, my observations in multiple fields taught me tremendous things which built my confidence in what I do for a living. Being on the ground post-Katrina, in the boardrooms and at conferences with both the wealthy and those who desire to be wealthy, has given me an advantage that I use in advising and strategizing for others. Everyone is an Avenger of some kind. We all have a superpower if we take the time to identify it. Your superpower, for instance, maybe as a doer, but you're acting in the capacity of a thinker. As you travel down The NarrowRoad, you'll find out how best to show up in the world to maximize your innate talent.

Through The NarrowRoad method, you will discover that wealth resides within you. This understanding leads to creating a more personal definition of wealth and a roadmap to pursue it. Consider the roadmap an invitation to chart a path toward the wealth you desire to create. Keep in mind that wealth is a group process that integrates individual and collective values, perspectives, strategies, life missions, and outcomes. To build wealth, a group must agree to create a system that links the past to the present and the future in ways that honor and reflect both the ideas and intentions of every member of the group. The desired outcome of wealth-building groups must be in the pursuit of legacy wealth; however, it has been defined. This will ensure that the commitment is not to an individual but to a collective outcome which time has finally come.

Legacy wealth intrigues me because there are elements of our lives that are, in a sense, hidden from our view. These dark places along our journey are gaps in our history, business (income) and financial (management) acumen. While they impact our pursuits of legacy wealth, we are blind to their measurable and meaningful existence. Navigating these dark places on our life's journey toward promise is this book's focus. I want you to see the path to where you believe your promise of legacy wealth resides.

Along my journey, I have found we suffer from blindness when it comes to looking down the road toward wealth. Our society has become a "right now" society, and waiting for things hoped for is not high on our priority lists. As a result, people no longer know how to build, grow, and expand upon what they really desire. This lack of long-term vision is so common today that it's not even looked upon as vision blindness, but rather as bad luck, the system's fault, or a wrong turn on the road toward legacy. The prevailing group myth that connecting dots or passing torches is not something to focus one's life on, shortens aspects of our reality, leaving a gap in the beam of awareness that defines our world from moment to moment.

Our world is a series of interconnected relationships with businesses, systems, finances, and cultures intertwined.

Consciously and unconsciously, these interactions occur every day and have historical context. I want to raise your awareness of this fact. I want to show you how to connect the ideas, dreams, missions, and collective purpose across generations, so that we can all journey this life, seeing what we believe.

My journey helped me define the specific focus for the narrative of this book and the narrative of my life. That focus is to guide the way to notice what we currently do not notice—the important role wealth plays in our life journey. Raising awareness will become a guide to noticing what we currently do not. The NarrowRoad can help you shine a flicker of light in the dark places or blind spots on life's journey. A blind spot is a physiological metaphor for our failure to see things as they are. In physiology, a blind spot is a gap in our field of vision resulting from the architecture of the eye. Ordinarily, what is missed by one eye is compensated for by overlapping vision of the other. This visual compensation is why we do not ordinarily notice our blind spots. However, when one eye is closed, the blind spot emerges. The blind spot in our individual and collective journeys is the closing of the doors between generations.

As I spoke with thousands of people about faith, finance, legacy, wealth, and the Promised Land, things were revealed to me on my journey. The responses from elders, adults, and youths taught me how to fully observe present situations. I came to understand that the dots must be connected between our past, present, and future to unearth the promises that exist in our personal lives, our legacies, and the business opportunities which reside within the two. Business along The NarrowRoad is a series of increasingly intimate relationships between our present life (and what we choose to make of it), and our past (the now inherited dreams and missions from those who have come before us), and to our future (that which lies further down the road). At this intersecting point, our inherited legacy business forms patterns.

I began looking for patterns within patterns, and a meta pattern emerged. We often fail to see meta patterns because few of us are taught to look for them. The NarrowRoad is my meta pattern. On one's wealth journey, these patterns are formed from a series of decisions one must make concerning their faith and finance—one which details the promise hidden in-between. This book strives to describe the pattern as clearly as possible.

The meta pattern I discovered became the methodology to develop The NarrowRoad. I've helped individuals identify their unique definition of the promise in their own backyard. I have used this tool with every client, in every keynote, and in every community on my Jolly-Journey, which I've been blessed to venture. Along this journey, it became clear that my grandmother was right: It is hard to see the full picture when you are posing for it. Finding a method for getting outside of oneself is the key to extending the length of vision to that of legacy wealth.

My research gave me the confidence to declare that for almost everyone on a journey, in terms of finance, both personal and collective, relationships with money reside in a dark place. The contrasting viewpoints and opinions about money became an emerging pattern repeated across race, gender, class, and religious affiliation.

For illustration purposes, let us accept the Bible as an instruction book with lessons on how people have navigated the times. The reality is that the lessons in this masterful book still apply. Historically then, we see that at each inflection point of the Israelites' journey through the wilderness to the biblically narrated Promised Land, that steps are repeated over and over again, and that this holds true throughout history. Their Promised Land represented an inherited opportunity that required taking risks and working with others to pursue and acquire. Emerging statistics concerning the wealth gap in current times show that the same promised land opportunities that should be available for everyone (equality, freedom, financial health, physical health, etc.), for certain groups in our land, i.e., African-American, there are risks associated with trying to take possession of their promise. Some groups see their promised land as a possibility, while others see it as a vision whose time has come.

Looking through this Promised Land lens, I noticed that with each major degree of freedom earned—income, class, independence, and investment—there was a dark place along the journey that needed the light of a torch. With each degree of freedom, we come closer to connecting the past, present, and future to inform our pursuit of the promise of true freedom, the way we have defined it for ourselves. As I reflected and gathered more evidence, the pattern became more focused and conclusive.

How This Book is Organized

The book is divided into parts 1 and 2. Part 1 is an explanation of The NarrowRoad origin and concept. The following fifteen chapters encompass both narrative and action plans. At the end of some chapters are questions meant to fully immerse and guide you on your journey along The NarrowRoad. On your journey, you will come to appreciate that legacy is wealth when considered a long-term investment that spans generations. The questions invite you to think strategically about the phases of your life as independent pursuits to a promise. Think of what you want and the ways that will effectively get you there. To accomplish your pursuits, if you do things your way, and according to your NarrowRoad Identity, you'll find that with a consistent budget of time, you'll navigate further down the road and ultimately out of the wilderness. Finally, this journey will assist in igniting the hidden treasure inside of you. It allows you to shine the light for generations, collectivity showing others that a realized promise in our lives is the reason we can't wait to make legacy wealth a reality. The NarrowRoad helps journeyers clarify their purpose. Life becomes more than income and expenses. It becomes a legacy that elevates its standard to wealth in perpetuity.

How to Use the Text

Skim it.

Take in the surface details to develop a sense of what is beneath the cover.

Ask what kind of companion you want to make of it.

Decide What The NarrowRoad is for You

- A text of wisdom that can enlighten you along your journey.
- A text of knowledge that can guide you to greater understanding.
- A text of key steps that can direct your need for results.
- A text of messages that can assist you in overcoming your fears.

The NarrowRoad strives to be all these things. The relationship you wish to have with it is up to you. Journey as you see fit and know your path to a deeper relationship with legacy and wealth begins here. Only you can define wealth for you and your family. Everyone's definition will be a little different. My goal is that you will enjoy wealth your way, and I am grateful you have chosen to begin your NarrowRoad journey. Enjoy!

PART 1

THE NARROWROAD OVERVIEW

*What matters less is what's on the page but
what's in your head as you read it.*

—Youngme Moon

The NarrowRoad, the byproduct of my search for my purpose, which combined my love of God, business, and people, emerged as a way forward to expand my knowledge and appreciation of wealth. As I'd soon come to learn, there are five forms of capital leading to wealth along The NarrowRoad—human, social, intellectual, cultural, and spiritual. My search revealed that we are more alike than not in our relationships with money and exchanging things of value regardless of our beginnings. Our legacy perspectives, molded and shaped by the people who came before us, influence the differences among us as a people. Our experiences are culturally unique, and cultural bias can create obstacles in our lives and influence our journey. Perhaps, if more people participated in the system of ownership, the bias as it currently exists could and would eventually change to a more balanced one—one more representative and understanding of both the value of hard work and the value of owning at least some part of the business around the work. If America is the land of the free, and you feel you are not, what specifically is stopping you? Is it the system or your lack of understanding of how to deploy the system in your favor? Perhaps unemployment or underemployment viewed in this way could be an invitation to declare your pursuit of independence. If the market rejects your efforts, build a medium of exchange in the market for yourself. You have value, and exchanging it can produce even more. Essentially, own your system for success in building wealth your way.

The Five Steps of The NarrowRoad

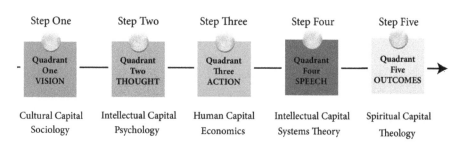

For example, voting is a hard-won battle for many—especially women and people of color. But voting, in a government-run system, can be an equalizer when we truly understand its impact on the system. As we all reflect on our collective right to vote, I encourage you to take the time to review: What is it that you desire to own with your gift of life? What liberties does that require you to take? And in light of these two strands: What does this mean for the direction of your pursuit? Be sure to invest the time to fully understand your position before casting a ballot against your own interest. It is, after all, your right to pursue your liberties here in America and to be successful. The choice always remains with you and what you desire to do with your five capitals to build legacy wealth. Voting gives you a voice for the things you desire for the collective.

I decided to spend time exploring the different perspectives that impact our journey. The answers to my questions appeared as glimpses of light shone on the dark places created during times of chaos, confusion, and doubt. These glimpses, which I refer to as our legacy perspectives, are what gave me eyes to see beyond what at first appeared to be the financial wilderness we all find ourselves when navigating in the beginning phases of our wealth journey. Exiting this wilderness is necessary to arrive at opportunities to pursue the faith-filled promises that often remain hidden within you and me. It is the road that resides beyond the financial wilderness that leads to the liberation of our talents. On the following pages I share my perspective of the glimpses I had of the hidden treasure that resides in all of us.

Thousands of people unknowingly shared with me the same fears and frustrations about their relationship with money. Many think it's only money that creates wealth. I created this book as a guide for the perplexed. It is for those uncertain about how to make the best choice from all the options and talents they've been given to arrive at their Promise—regardless of race, culture or creed.

As you read this book, you will begin your journey down The NarrowRoad. Consider this first journey as a guide through the principles of The NarrowRoad that will reveal a path unique to you for obtaining your wealth. This is significant because a tool to wealth like this has never been available before. The reality is that in most of our lives, The NarrowRoad is one that few find and even fewer take.

On the journey to discovering my life's purpose, three things became clear:

1. Wealth is created every day in America by businesses and their owners who know simple principles.
2. For too many regular people, legacy is something talked about in small groups and at funerals, while for the wealthy, it is something studied, owned, focused on, and passed forward.
3. Faith is the one thing that either unifies or is leveraged by everybody when finances are tight and legacies have been forgotten.

When attempting to pursue wealth, a concept far beyond finances, many beliefs must be understood. This can seem overwhelming. My advice is to follow the wise suggestions of those who came before you: approach each text, each set of suggestions, as if a new acquaintance. Build relationships with each step of the journey to help narrow the road to wealth your way.

What Exactly Is The NarrowRoad?

Enter through the narrow gate. For wide is the gate, and broad is the road that leads to destruction, and many enter through it. But small is the gate and narrow the road that leads to life, and only a few find it.

—**Matthew 7:13–14** *(New International Version)*

We play various roles along our life journey—visionary, thinker, doer, speaker, and deliverer of outcomes. Our dominant role is how we authentically show up in the world and is the role most likely to get us to the Promised Land. Inauthenticity usually comes with an itch that won't let us rest until scratched.

The NarrowRoad system, a roadmap, helps anyone discover the unique thought processes that govern their lives. For example, I'm best able to process things through observations. My observations in financial services, strategy, investments, entrepreneurship, and theology have helped build my confidence in what I do for a living.

Your true superpower may be as a doer, but you may find yourself struggling in the right room, performing in the wrong role, trying to show up in the world as a thinker. The unrest between who you are authentically and what you do, if different, can be a roadblock to your progress. The beauty of this tool is that you'll find that out as you travel along The NarrowRoad.

The Five Quadrants of The NarrowRoad

Quadrant Three	IMPERSONAL REALITY WITH MONEY	Quadrant Four
Human / Financial Capital		Social Capital
Above Ground ACTION	Quadrant Five	SPEECH
Below Ground THOUGHT	Spiritual Capital	VISION
Quadrant Two	INTANGIBLE YET TRANSFERABLE ASPECTS OF MONEY AND WEALTH	Quadrant One
Intellectual Capital		Cultural Capital

The most preferred way to deliver outcomes is through partnerships and alliances. Similar to Jesus sending the disciples aligned with his vision for change out in twos. We can also best deliver when paired with someone of complementary expertise who shares the vision we are pursuing. This is why along the journey (should you choose to accept my invitation), you'll be introduced to co-builders of solutions custom-tailored for you.

This may not make much sense to you now but will become clear in the chapters to follow. On our journey in exploring The NarrowRoad system, you'll come to appreciate that systems are neutral and that it is people who are biased. Your particular bias on The NarrowRoad comes from your NarrowRoad Identity. You will also come to know, and hopefully, love the dimensions of your NRID and how it enriches your relationships with others, with money, and with what and how you believe in that which gave you your unique point of view. The answers to the key questions asked reveal what is true to you. The system then exposes a narrative based on your answers that, when understood, guides you further down the road to the life you most desire. This is how your NRID becomes a system that reveals your true wealth identity.

Who is The NarrowRoad For?

I wrote this book for six audiences:

- Visionaries who have the wisdom but not the knowledge of the resources necessary to build legacy wealth;
- Thinkers who have the knowledge but not the strategy and confidence to build legacy wealth;
- Doers who have the understanding of the work required to create wealth but not the understanding of the business around the work to create wealth for themselves;

- Speakers who have the passion and love for community, friends, and family but not the systems and structures to exchange and build wealth with those who matter most to them;
- Anyone who desires to be met where they are, financially and otherwise, and guided to where they wish to go.
- The utterly perplexed.

Along your journey, you'll find twenty-four unique identities within The NarrowRoad, and there is one custom-tailored for you. The specific way you function as a visionary, thinker, doer and speaker is unique to you. Building a better relationship with the ways and means in which you function in these four roles is how you discover your wealth identity. My dream with writing this book is that anyone and everyone who desires to live life more abundantly learns the best method to do so. I believe The NarrowRoad and understanding your unique NRID will help.

Let's begin our journey down The NarrowRoad. We will narrow our focus to the following four key things to build wealth as a legacy:

- Write your legacy wealth vision and anchor your life to it.
- Take the time to make the vision plain and believe in it.
- Address the dark places in your life that require understanding. Get clarity and the details needed to get you beyond the patterns that disrupt your journey.
- Face your fears so that your life speaks its truth.

Why a NarrowRoad?

We all seek direction in life—a way to go forward toward the things we want most. *The Good News* found in Matthew 7:14

speaks of the wide gate of options we are presented with in life. The text suggests a direction we should go, and it further refers to a NarrowRoad that leads to a life that only a few will find. When this biblical text found me, it confirmed that The Narrow-Road I was on would lead to the journey to create this guide, which in turn could help many discover their NarrowRoad to the life they envision.

In my research, I found many young people were frustrated with the older generations because elders are often fond of telling *what* they did in "their day" but tended to shy away from the details of *how*. The younger generation has far more interest in the how. How did their forebearers reach such great heights? How can their success be replicated and carried forward? I can relate. In my experiences with mentors who'd broken barriers and surpassed what others thought impossible, I saw that they were reluctant to share certain specifics. I now understand that implicit elements of one's unique identity are embedded in the explicit details of the *how* of success. As a result, future generations are left out of the stories that enable them to pick up the torch and move it further down the road to another level of success.

The truth, and the whole truth, needs to be shared within and across generations for wealth to become a legacy. Let's imagine life as a highway. Each of us enters it on different generational ramps. It's highly likely that each will take the lane prioritized by their life choices to get to the desired destination.

Some of us go fast. Others stay within the mandated speed limit. Some may even go slower than allowed. Others may start and stop or turn around. We may even have taken the wrong lane or met a detour on our journey. As we enter The Narrow(er) Road, we will soon discover if we are in the correct lane or even on the right road to reach life's desired outcomes.

The NarrowRoad uses the unconscious, but well-intentioned, mistakes of purpose-driven people seeking wealth. While traveling along life's journey, hoping to recalibrate the roadmap that allows them full ownership of the talents and opportunities presented, they stumble. These mistakes are what I refer to as those parts of the road that are dark, rough terrains that influences leaving or taking possession of an inheritance. This in-between distance from here to there is where we must narrow our focus. When the journey to wealth is pursued with a wide-angled view, it is often the unconscious and costly mistakes that delay passing the torch of Promise from one generation to the next. Correcting or avoiding these mistakes requires an in-depth understanding of faith, finance, and a willingness to explore the depth of who you are and where you truly desire to go in the window of time life offers.

The ideas and strategies you'll be privy to along The Narrow-Road will help you clarify your position. You will discover emerging, discernable patterns that will help mitigate and lessen the mistakes in your pursuit. If more individuals were aware of their life purpose earlier, their world would become what was promised much sooner. As a result, the collective world would become more fruitful. With increased awareness, enlightenment shows us that we don't have to run the first leg of the road alone and cover every obstacle. Those before us have already covered so much ground. Lives before us were lived in pursuit of us getting further down the road, and we simply have to unearth the cues and clues. I've stated before that wealth is a group and generational process. I will restate this throughout the book because the concept is one that is imperative to grasp. There is truly no need to go through the darkness alone. Those before us have left a torch to get us to the full light of your life. Those in waiting will help us in the present moment.

In order to navigate the inevitable financial wilderness and to claim the promised inheritance in the land of opportunity, it's necessary to identify the tribe that has helped or can help you get to what is important to you. Pursuing the promise requires a solid foundation of knowing and believing that what *is* for you *is for you*, because it is promised. Enlightenment is what puts you on The NarrowRoad where a more in-depth awareness of legacy becomes the fuel for life's purpose and is what lights our path through the wilderness. Clarity allows you to spend less time wandering in the financial wilderness and more time unearthing the inherited hidden treasure you already own. Imagine no more wasting time living from moment to moment or paycheck-to-paycheck because you're unaware of what has been passed on as your inheritance. The NarrowRoad method gives us a pathway to claim the promised inheritance and the tools to pass the torch on to the generations.

Collective change takes forty years. Forty years mark the beginning and the end of an era. Living to see the Promise is possible when generations are connected across the wilderness and know what to look for to pursue life's purpose. I have found that this level of *knowing* is most needed to arrive at the Promised Land as defined by your legacy. Taking possession of the Promise requires vision, strategy, mission, a system of expression and defined outcomes. When combined with wise leadership and generational stewardship, all of these factors finance the creation, pursuit, and ongoing operations needed to maintain and attain the Promise. Let me get a bit more specific here about finance versus wealth. Finance, by definition, is the allocation of *assets* and *liabilities* over time under conditions of certainty and uncertainty. A key point in monetary finance is the *time value of money*, which states that a unit of currency today is worth more than the same unit of currency tomorrow.

This is why we cannot wait to focus on the pursuit of our Promise. Owning life assets, both inherited and created, is the way to finance the pursuit of our Promise. The certainty of the biblical narrative is that once the Promised Land is attained, the real journey begins.

I observed the patterned viewpoints my desires created. I deeply desire a more perfect union between freedom and the creation of more successful pathways in its pursuit. I am not the first. In the Bible, Abraham sought a perfect union with God. President Lincoln sought a more perfect union between the North and the South. Dr. Martin Luther King, Jr., a man who self-identified as a Moses, sought a more perfect union between America and her promise. Former President Barack Obama declared his time in office as a Joshua era, a succession of Dr. King if you will, as he sought to advance a more perfect union between a black and white America and greater inclusion of people into the middle-class. Again, this shows the need to connect generations. In the biblical narrative of the promised land, Moses led his people out of slavery into the wilderness. But it was Joshua, two generations later, who picked up the torch and led the people out of the wilderness into the Promised Land. The lessons then and now follow a pattern that connects the generational dots to form a path towards wealth that is promised.

The Interconnected Pillars of The NarrowRoad

- Unity
- Agreement
- Group Decisions
- Freedom

Unity, agreement, and group decisions allowed the Israelites to overcome the fear of giants in their land of promise to attain freedom. Unity brought victory to the North to overcome the resistance in the South. Unity forced America to see that segregation was not in alignment with her Promise. Finally, it was unity that Americans needed to support the audacity to hope that there was "change we could all believe in" when the nation voted the first Black man to the Presidency of the United States. It will be unity that will allow us to overcome and fully attain the Promise of One Nation Under God.

The future of America, given its complicated history of unequal systemic design, hinges on the belief that we are one nation under God—all of us given from a God who makes good on His promises. Within the melting pot of our collective, there is an abundance of hidden treasure, ideas, hopes, and dreams that have lost connections across seas, time and spaces. The nature of the American tapestry needs to be a singular mission and purpose to call these dry bones together. Our pursuits of Promise depend on it.

My research has made me confident of this fact—great wealth lies just beneath the surface of our current situations if only we had a way, and the courage, to unite what we want with what we believe. The pursuit of life, liberty, and ownership are not just the American Dream. These pursuits are part of everyone's journey. From the Israelites' pursuit of the Promised Land to the desire of the Founding Fathers of America for a great nation, to the emancipated slave's desire for equity and ownership. Those journeys all began with the pursuit of freedom.

When the dots of the past, present, and future are not connected, a legacy pursuit resembles "grasshoppers wandering in the wilderness" rather than inheritors of a Promise. For the Israelites, it was the second generation that was organized enough to go out from the wilderness as spies to survey the Promised Land. Of the many groups deployed, only two groups came back believing it was possible to reach the Promised Land. The others remarked they were only grasshoppers to the giants who presently inhabited the Promised Land, and success would not be possible. They did not understand that a grasshopper's legs store up energy to escape danger, and if humans could jump the way grasshoppers did, they could jump the length of a football field.

A disconnected perspective of who we are across generations robs us of meaning, purpose, and identity. It works to dilute our understanding of how to leave inheritances that create consistent wealth for generations to come, which is a core element of the journey to the Promised Land. As a result, many of us start from scratch leaving behind hidden treasures in our pursuit of wealth. To fully come into our possession, each successive generation must remember the promise. Life allows each generation to elevate their inherited standard of legacy to wealth, however they define it. Looking at our lives this way is not unheard of, but I've found it is not consistent in our communities.

Within unity comes another degree of freedom, and with each degree of freedom comes a different dimension of wealth. The meta pattern of The NarrowRoad makes this plain. It allows us to clearly see what is hidden within the in-between: faith, finance, and wealth.

Freedom, as a result, is the ability to navigate beyond the financial wilderness by using the resources available to make choices that allow us to take possession of our promise in the manner we desire.

Faith is the currency that connects what is, to what is promised and the glue that holds the pillars together. Unity, which leads to agreement and group decisions, leads to the change required to attain freedom.

I believe that now is the best time to get a clearer vision of the unique NarrowRoad. It will lead to the land we as Americans have been promised, exactly the way we have defined. Faith played a central role at the beginning of this American Journey as this was designed to be one great nation under God.

We will now chart your path to legacy wealth along The NarrowRoad as designed by you. I have elected to use biblical and historical narratives of the Promised Land to unite the capitals of one's wealth identity with society's ongoing pursuit of the American Dream. The Promised Land biblical narrative is familiar regardless of faith, tradition, race, or ethnicity, largely due to Reverend Dr. Martin Luther King, Jr.'s use during the march on Washington and in speeches throughout the Civil Rights movement. It has become a guiding narrative for the past two and a half generations. Over fifty years ago, Dr. King declared he'd seen the Promised Land and believed that one day America would arrive at that place of promise where equality was the right of all. His long-term vision was not equally shared by all who heard his declaration. However, long-term vision is a requirement for declarations of equality, independence, financial or otherwise. Often, many are not in agreement with such declarations. Yet the promise of the declaration remains and will be fulfilled. For those who can see and hear and are ready to fulfill the promise, The NarrowRoad provides a roadmap for success.

This book is an invitation to join a journey along The NarrowRoad to define and build wealth your way. The accompanying summary primer (located at the end of some chapters) is to enlighten each journeyer along The NarrowRoad. It will help you see that legacy is wealth when considered a long-term investment that spans generations. The questions in the primer invite you to think strategically about phases of your life. Once you understand The NarrowRoad and its principles, you can begin the journey and chart a path toward your legacy wealth. Should you desire to go further along The NarrowRoad, I have created a collective space for wealth builders to learn and grow called the Wealth Finishing School. We need to put something at the end of the book as promise.

The foundation of legacy wealth is what we will explore in this book. In the end, you will come away with your unique definition that can be passed on to future generations to be shaped and customized as all navigate further down the road. Why is this important? As noted earlier, the distance between the elder generation's knowledge of what to do, and the younger rising generation's desire to do, is a little word—*how*. Younger people are not satisfied with what you did or even why it was done. To believe they can pick up the torch and carry the dream forward, they need to understand the how. Unfortunately, the how is what gets lost in translation, fading into memory, and lost to the legacy story. However you choose to define it, the ultimate destination of The NarrowRoad is legacy wealth, your sphere of influence and your community.

Your successful wealth-life is a snapshot of the reconnection of your legacy. It contains the hopes and dreams of generations past coming to fruition. Your lifestyle sends messages for all the world to hear and ultimately see the promises you have inherited. Your life is a message that speaks more truth than many of us realize.

Your journey to the Promised Land starts here. Promises have dimensions. The road to Promise is unique. Not everyone will choose to go through each dimension of the Promise in their lifetime, and this is why legacy narratives are so important. Letting your life speak to the values and victories of your pursuit is only half the story. The wealth you pursued and created along The NarrowRoad of legacy wealth is a series of choices. Some choices are unconsciously made when the narrative you have inherited is not your starting blueprint. The extent to which you leave a legacy narrative helps those coming behind you make similar, if not better, decisions to further the possession of yet another dimension of the promise.

An Important Distinction to Note as You Work Through the Questions in This Book

Financial wealth is attained by journeying through a series of financial decisions that build and grow over time via savings and investments.

Legacy wealth is a narrative that did not start with us. Nor will it end with us unless we discontinue the conversation across generations—an act that would stop the passing of the torch of wisdom, knowledge, and evolving understanding. Legacy wealth integrates the past with the present and prepares us for the future our ancestors promised. Legacy wealth is an individual pursuit of life purpose, rolled up into the collaborative journey with generational, communal, national, and global implications. Legacy wealth is so much more than money, yet too few take the time to own this reality. I am grateful that it is no longer you.

PART 2

Chapter One

OUR HISTORY

History serves as the context through which we ground the commonalities Americans all share in the pursuit of Legacy Wealth. History and prophecy are integrated into one powerful narrative. There are two references to a promise in the Bible—the Old Testament, which speaks of a future time, and the New Testament, which often reflects on a prior time. Christianity, Judaism, Islam—all documented faiths stem from the same source—God's promise to Abraham, a man who chose to follow God and believe in His promises. We all serve an important role in history. Whether to move the lever forward, from survival to freedom for ourselves and others. Or to move beyond freedom to new heights of awareness. Awareness of what is possible, what is necessary, and what is needed—a truly united America (The Promised Land).

It is in this way that our history is one of the best teachers about wealth and purpose. There are patterns in history that can remind us of where we are, where we are going, and what needs our attention. As a result, the road we are traveling in our lifetime is smoother than the road traveled by those before us. History is prophecy if we care to listen and see the patterns that inform.

One of the most pivotal books I read along my journey was *Generations* by Neil Howe and William Strauss. Strauss and Howe, two brilliant historians and strategists, journeyed back to the 1500s and studied the connections between generations. The authors posit a pattern of four repeating phases, generational types, and a recurring cycle of spiritual awakenings and secular crises from the founding colonials to the present day. History essentially repeats itself every four generations.

They created a predictive model from this research and wrote a second book called *The Fourth Turning*. This masterful work centered on the discovery that generations move in constellations or patterns called saeculums. Their research further revealed that every fourth generation repeats a cycle of life. Each generation's contribution to the ongoing narrative keeps the wheel of the world moving forward. That narrative impacts a span of more than two hundred years. Four generations of ideas, dreams, missions, and lived purpose make up the world as we know it today. This book used history as a springboard to predict what would happen next in our "future" history. *The Fourth Turning* was written about "right now" more than twenty-five years ago, so we have some perspective for comparison. It's remarkable how accurate they were in detailing how our society would reach a point of crisis and meltdown so that it could build itself back up again. We have seen this. The book also validates that there is nothing new under the sun.

All we need to do is observe where we are today to validate their theory. Things are crumbling all around us. Our economy reveals the cracks and breakage in its system, calling attention to what we must address as a nation. Our financial services industry is revealing its need for more accountability and focus on all levels. Failure in our government is revealing the need for greater citizen participation to encourage a more perfect union. As with the Israelites, it was Joshua, not Moses, who led the pursuit of the Promised Land, and it was the third generation, not the second, that followed suit, and the fourth that delivered the Promised Land. This is an inflection point for our nation. We are in the "fourth turning" with the opportunity to effect change and deliver on the promise. One generation is now nearing the end of its reign, leaving it up to the next two generations to determine the next leg of the journey, and the Promise is inevitable!

Delays in the inevitable are not denials to a promise whose time has not yet come. My love of research, history, and these two aforementioned books, have enlightened my journey. They have given me the ability to see key patterns in our history. Patterns that reveal the importance of going back far enough to pick up deferred dreams of the past that have already been fertilized in the pursuits of those before us and are now ready for harvest.

This generational pattern throughout history repeats over and over. Once we understand its principles, we can take appropriate action. There is nothing wrong with dreaming big. Big dreams are what have gotten us through the stuck points in history. A big dream that still impacts our world today came from the erudite dreamer Dr. Martin Luther King, Jr. His dream left a fifty-year imprint in our historical memories. Like his biblical mentor, Moses, King spoke of a Promised Land that he had the privilege of catching a glimpse of but would not get there with us to see its full promise. Dr. King's pursuit of the big dream of freedom ultimately led to a life, however short, in pursuit of a purpose of economic equality for all people in America. Near the end of his life, when he reviewed the expanse navigated,

Dr. King remarked he felt he'd led his people into the "burning house" discovered on the road traveled.

The pattern of history reveals purpose if you take the time to connect the dots. History will be your teacher throughout your NarrowRoad journey. Together we will connect the dots. They will reveal the choices and decisions you must make to navigate beyond the financial wilderness. The NarrowRoad views history as a valley of dry bones. When called together, bones can breathe life and build a mighty army for you to pursue your purpose within your window of opportunity.

Our lives span four generations. A generation is roughly twenty-two years. Our window of opportunity to influence and contribute financially to the movement of history is often condensed into forty years. We must navigate through the financial wilderness for two generations to build up the necessary reserve, to fund the possession of a promise we have each uniquely inherited.

The New Testament consists of letters ranging from believers who were dreamers, to believers who wanted to actualize the promise of the dreams in their communities. These letters, or gospels, were good news that believers navigating the wilderness of life could reflect upon. Gospels shared the history of what happened so the hearers of the Word could believe in what would eventually come to pass because it was promised. History does not change, but we can change our perspective of the value of our history. We can use it as good news to chart our path and to prove our concept that the lives of others represented in the present day are equally valuable. The good news informs future generations.

Building a reserve to fund the possession of the Promised Land in our lifetime is not just composed of money. Money is just time multiplied by a wage. Time is also converted into other currencies that are equally, if not more valuable. Throughout The NarrowRoad journey, we will explore all the currencies available to you and ways you can best exchange them to navigate your unique wilderness path to the promise you have chosen to spend your life pursuing.

Whether you represent a first, second, third, or fourth generation, we are all on this journey together. As history promises, the best is always yet to come. Those with audacity know that some dreams have been deferred. They take the time to learn about those past dreams to create advantages for their visions. I'm one of those people, and you are a beneficiary of the results of my legacy wealth pursuit. It is in this way that the legacy narrative continues. Let us journey further down the road together and pick up a torch or two to light the path of prophetic history.

In the book, *The Fourth Turning*, the authors remark that "history, once understood, can be prophecy." I have seen this to be true throughout my Jolly-Journey. We are all on individual and collective journeys to pursue the promise of life as desired. This has been, and always will be. I reached out to the authors of *The Fourth Turning* while working in New Orleans. I shared my love for the book with Mr. Howe and asked questions concerning the African-American community. At the time of Hurricane Katrina, five generations of African-Americans had lived in New Orleans, the oldest inhabited place in America. Did that mean what we saw post-Katrina, was the beginnings of a new turn of the wheel?

"Katrina was a sign of things to come," Mr. Howe said. "Rebuilding post-Katrina would be fruitful for the journey that lies ahead for all Americans," Howe further admitted that their research was not as vast on the history of African-Americans and that it would be of great benefit to explore their unique history, as I aimed to use their predictive model to chart a path for communities of color. I saw the history of African-Americans as a useful prophetic guide for all Americans. The history of the African-American's journey is directly connected to my history and the history of America's business model. I saw then, and believe now, that the business condition of African-Americans reflects on the business progress of America. Like it or not, the pursuit of equality in America is consistently sparked by the legacy narrative of the Black community. This is a perspective you will learn along The NarrowRoad. The brief conversation with Mr. Howe left an impression on me. History of all types—American, biblical, African-American, and business—became the foundation of every journey along The NarrowRoad.

Our founding fathers believed it was the providence of God that allowed them to forge a declaration and constitution that created one united nation, a country of vast differences, with one shared dream to build a nation that was democratic and free. Their belief system acknowledged the need for order, shared governance, and a commitment to wealth creation. This wilderness journey had been exacting and, for some, quite inequitable, yet the journey, like the wheel of life, continues.

In my travels through several communities, I begin to ask myself, "What knits us together?" My answer: History. Specifically, business history and American history, so that's where we should start. After all, this nation is a business (a legacy business), and we are all inheritors of its promise. The promise of business, when pursued successfully, is wealth; wealth creation through ownership of the time, talent, and subsequent treasure found in the field of opportunity called life pursued in a terrain called a market. We all share this history. Few understand it completely. Even fewer will ever attain it. For history to be prophecy, the dots of wisdom, knowledge, and understanding must be connected to wealth creation. In America, we must strive to connect all the historical dots of *all* its citizens so that the long-overdue act of balancing the equation of equality through unity can be solved.

I began asking the following questions in 2008: If Reverend Dr. Martin Luther King, Jr., in 1968, spoke of his dream of the Promised Land, and forty years later, presidential candidate, Barack Obama, picked up his torch and began his campaign by stating that we are in a Joshua generation, then from our American sociopolitical context, what is the Promised Land? How do we get there together? How do we fund the pursuit? What, if anything, needs to be learned to feel more confident while on the collective and individual journey to pursue the Promised Land? And how will we get this diverse nation to rise to the challenge together? I looked back at history to see what clues the legacy and teachings offered us.

Within the theological underpinnings of the Israelites story, the Promised Land was an inheritance to take possession of by Moses' people. Inheritance implies ownership. The invitation to build an enterprise that can sustain future generations once outside the bonds of wandering in the wilderness and Egyptian slavery. Ownership is the possession of equity. This biblical narrative indicates that in the case of the Israelites, at the end of their long, multigenerational journey, emergent communities only took possession of ten percent of their inheritance. Akin to the notion that we humans only use ten percent of our brainpower. There is so much more available to us if we only know how to access it and take possession. The promise of wealth is no different; it's a group process.

Therein lies the primary lesson in the pursuit of a Promised Land. There is a need for a connected understanding of how to take full possession of a promise. How does one link an idea of freedom to a promise of equality? What lies hidden in this question are the keys to wealth creation. Is it necessary to align our mission in life, with an understanding of its purpose, in relation to a promise that spans generations? Is this then how we, as individuals, let our light shine and reflect upon the collective? If yes, then the access we need is our legacy and its pursuit of wealth. The good news is that when we prioritize this aspect of our wealth vision, in many ways, we already have it.

This is what I sought to uncover on my Jolly-Journey—a way for us to uniquely define ourselves so that collectively we can take possession of our promises by valuing each other. The keys I found along the road are embedded within The Narrow-Road method. You unlock the keys to your promise once you go through the entry gate of The NarrowRoad, which reveals your wealth identity, your NRID.

Searching for a way to address the tensions between the systems of business, and the structures of faith, ignited my prophetic imagination. I began to consider the sacred narrative of the Promised Land as a call to take possession of ancestral promises in our backyards. Within the pursuit of the Promised Land resides a forty-year delay, a concept I will discuss at length later in the book. As things became clear on my Jolly-Journey, it erased my confusion about why we were waiting to pursue our Promised Land. The pursuit is collective according to the wisdom found in the biblical narrative of the Promised Land. We are supposed to go together. America has not yet united. To get to the Promise, we must navigate out of the wilderness *in standards* like the Israelites. This means that each tribal group assigned specific assignments and tasks while in the wilderness, as part of the collective journey, must complete their mission to attain the Promise that awaits. Very much like a business assigns tasks to its varying groups of workers in departments to reach its overall goal, American citizens must recognize and respect the role each of us plays in getting to the Promise. This has not been easy for most Americans, so we continue to wander in the wilderness of possibilities. The tumult of the Trump era has shown us that a real opportunity to move toward unity exists. If each tribe shares in the harvest of the Promise, we will move the torch a significant way along the journey toward individual freedoms.

Where are the groups to tip your scale? Who is in your tribe? What lies in the specific land of your promise? Which battles have you faced? Which ones will you fight? Which ones have you overcome? What is your inherited win?

How can we assist one another on this journey to take full possession of our unique promise amid our collective promise? Is this promise indeed unique to each of us? These are questions that will be answered along The NarrowRoad. History points to the answers to these questions if the time is taken to see the patterns. As we go forward, there are some concepts you will need to understand when traveling along The NarrowRoad. Here are some key things to remember:

> **Legacy Wealth**—Promises take time. Time to discern, create, build, grow, and expand to the next generation. My journey has revealed that Promises are more than worth the wait.
>
> Legacy and wealth are partners. Pursuing The NarrowRoad is how you will unite the two.

Faith, when unblinded, becomes a currency that reveals the abundant promise that exists for each and every one of us. Unblinded faith possesses both the substance and evidence of what we hope to obtain.

Wealth is a journey—the narrative that is a gift passed from one generation to the next to build opportunities via ownership.

Unity is the key to wealth and the glue that binds all the premises above—if you want to go fast, go alone, but if you want to go far, you must go together. The collective is far more powerful than the individual in reaching the promised land.

Promised Land is the vision we hold for our individual and collective lives.

Freedom comes in four degrees or levels of emancipation—work/income, lifestyle/class, growth/independence and expansion/influence.

Independence is a strategy you believe in enough to execute regardless of what others may think or do with or without you. An independent position along The NarrowRoad is step three—the decision to do what you want to do confidently because you can afford it.

NRID is your NarrowRoad identity and consists of a unique sequence of the four roles of a wealth builder. When you apply your NRID to your pursuit of wealth along The NarrowRoad it becomes your wealth identity— a tool to unblind your faith and activate your financial acumen.

Chapter Two

ENTERING THE NARROWROAD: KEY REQUIREMENTS ALONG THE NARROWROAD

Clarifying one's purpose in life begins with anchoring to an outcome you desire—the attainment of your Promised Land. Once your life is linked to an outcome, your purpose becomes manageable, more visible, and more of a promise than a possibility. The road to wealth your way becomes one you believe in.

To enter The NarrowRoad, the first question that needs to be answered is: What is it that you desire first and foremost?

Which of the following best describes your most immediate outcome?

I desire:

- To move beyond survival; no more living from paycheck to paycheck.
- To define freedom my way by living a lifestyle I can comfortably manage and enjoy throughout my lifetime.

- To move beyond socially accepted freedom and grow to a level of financial independence defined by my independent choices.
- To plan how best to leave wealth that expands my legacy wealth narrative for generations.

Clarifying One's Purpose Along The NarrowRoad

Each of the four outcomes relies on the other before and after it to succeed.

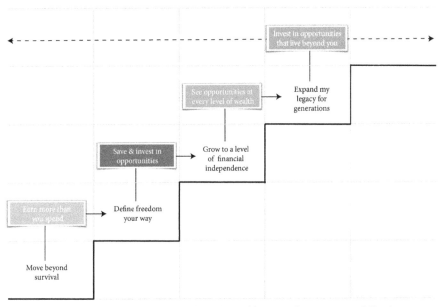

Once your life is linked to an outcome you desire, the road to wealth your way becomes one you believe in.

Legacy wealth is the promise we are after. Each of the outcomes listed above relies on the one before it, and after it, to succeed. To move beyond survival, one must earn more than one spends, which requires greater consumption from those free to create more income-earning opportunities. To move beyond freedom, one must learn how to save and invest in opportunities created by those planning long term for their not-so-plainly-seen future. To leave wealth that passes on for generations, one must be able to see opportunities in all the dimensions of wealth evolving along the way, following in the footsteps of those who came before us and leaving footsteps for those who are coming after us.

When viewed along your NarrowRoad, wealth creation is a series of financial decisions that build, grow, and expand over time with protected savings, ownership, and investments and is a precursor to legacy wealth. Your wealth journey contains many options that result in choices that require decisions you must make to get where you desire to go (and remain) along The NarrowRoad. Many of us need a roadmap to see the road we are on, to determine if it's the best road to take. Your NarrowRoad wealth journey starts with anchoring the end of your current situation to an outcome you choose.

Assignment—Entering The NarrowRoad

The NarrowRoad unique business system (custom-tailored for you) will emerge once you answer the one simple "entry gate" question of outcome and evaluate your current financial and life situation. To go further down The NarrowRoad, please answer the additional entry gate question. You can do this in one of two ways:

1. Visit www.mynarrowroad.com/entrygate and listen to the guided meditation that will help you reveal your NarrowRoad ID.

2. Uncover your NRID manually. Take a moment and close your eyes. Take a few deep breaths. Turn off your thoughts and emotions. Take a few more breaths and travel down to the core of who you are. Anchor yourself to the source of your inner confidence, the place where your inner voice

speaks. Once peacefully there, I want you to answer the following question without thinking or feeling. Answer from the inner knowing within you: Where do I go from here?

The NarrowRoad Entry Gate

There are four roles in the NRID Method to help best understand how to take greater ownership of the wealth builder in you. Your NRID helps you better understand how to navigate your independent journey in the world: as a visionary, a thinker, a doer, and a speaker.

What is your strongest role, second strongest, third, and fourth? Write them down as they come to you. Trust what you hear. Place your responses below on the left, and then match each role with the appropriate number on the right.

Place your response to the entry gate question here: _____

Enter The NarrowRoad

Rank each role #1 - #4 Strongest - Weakest	
RANK ORDER	ROLES
	THINKER
	DOER
	VISIONARY
	SPEAKER

DOER	SPEAKER
#3	#4
#2	#1
THINKER	VISIONARY

Congratulations! You have officially entered The NarrowRoad. The NarrowRoad method will now assist journeyers in charting a path toward their life purpose. It builds a roadmap for your unique life business and confirms that your direction is the right direction. The underlying premise is that anchoring to a wealth outcome helps to clarify your purpose by narrowing your focus to the steps, that with faith, you will take to achieve your ultimate desires for your life.

Enter The NarrowRoad

Rank each role #1 - #4 Strongest - Weakest	
RANK ORDER	ROLES
1	THINKER
2	DOER
3	VISIONARY
4	SPEAKER

DOER	SPEAKER
#3 V	#4 S
#2 D	#1 T
THINKER	VISIONARY

Each of the twenty-four NRID profiles is associated with a unique system for success that gets you to your ideal finish line. Looking at the illustration above, this journeyer is a thinker-visionary, doer-thinker, visionary-doer, and pure speaker. In their prioritized order, her roles are thinker, doer, visionary, speaker. Her identity reveals itself in the following ways:

1. Quadrant One: As a thinker-visionary, she is a strategic leader who first sees everything in her head. She is able

to see the next opportunity before most. Her blind spots are now ongoing and long-term, but if you need a thought leader, she is your girl.

2. Quadrant Two: As a doer-thinker, she is a practical, tactical independent thinker who must go out on her own to figure things out to confidently pursue her dreams. Experiences are her best teacher.

3. Quadrant Three: As a visionary-doer, she is most talented in the areas of developing others and seeing potential in ideas that have yet to come to fruition. She is easily paid to oversee operations of people and projects that have a lot of moving parts.

4. Quadrant Four: As a pure speaker, she is intense in her communication style; her emotions influence who she speaks with and what she says. Her triggers are found in words both said and unsaid.

5. These four outcomes align with her identity in that her number one focus is the near term. She is most confident in the immediate opportunities where she can be hands-on and the quickest when she can see what is happening. She is most connected to those she listens to and who listen to her.

Along The NarrowRoad, the Ultimate Desired Outcome Is Legacy Wealth

Our journey along The NarrowRoad is in the pursuit of wealth, happiness and promise; however we individually choose to define it. After talking with thousands of people, I'm convinced that each and every one of us is here, in this time and space, for a unique reason. A reason that did not begin with nine months in the womb and a series of pushes, but long before, by the generations who came before us. Our ultimate desired outcome is to create a legacy for ourselves which requires belief in our ability to connect the dots across generations and the confidence that we can and will do better than those who came before us. This is how legacy and wealth meet one another within our lifetime along The Narrow-Road. Each generation's purpose is to live a fun-filled, meaningful life, multiply the fruits of their efforts, and become resources for the next generation to take further down the eternal road.

As you enter the road, you'll notice that wide is the gate to destruction, as the biblical text suggests. Right actions done in the wrong sequence can cause so much damage. It destroys your confidence, devalues your talents and allows you to speak against the desires of your heart because of fear. For these reasons, many wander around these stuck points in the wilderness for years. Things could start out great and then loop back into chaos, confusion, avoidance, and an unfulfilled life and promise. Mistakes further dim your vision in the dark places you can't yet understand.

As the road narrows from the choices made, you will note, "Small Is the Gate & Narrow the Road," which invites you to define, create, build and grow wealth your way. Looking through the unique lens that is culturally biased by the legacy narratives you inherited, you will grow confident about the opportunities found along your NarrowRoad designed to sharpen the skills of your pursuit. You'll appreciate how to create the income needed to fuel the fire of the business of you by unearthing your talents and deploying them wisely. Building the life you desire requires sharing the load of getting to freedom with others who are willing to engage in your truth. The narrative created by these identity-specific statements becomes your roadmap of the life you desire.

Even on The NarrowRoad, only a few find the narrowest road to their ultimate fulfillment because, like my grandmother, Bessie Pearl Horne, would say, "It's hard to see the full picture when you are posing for it." Hard to see it, hard to believe it, consistently pursue it, grasp its reflection, and hard to admit that the full picture of your legacy wealth includes so much more than you. Remember seeing is believing, so once clear, belief in self will take you to The NarrowRoad that is uniquely created by you and evidenced with your roadmap. Your roadmap integrates the four quadrants of Vision, Thought, Action, and Speech into a pathway that becomes custom-tailored to you when applied to your identity and anchored to outcomes you believe are worth pursuing.

Steps Along The NarrowRoad

A business is a series of valued exchanges that, when connected, form a chain that builds in scale and scope over time. The larger the desired outcome, the larger the business system. Along The NarrowRoad are steps that create a personal business system for success. Owning your steps along the way is how the system becomes custom-tailored to you. Once connected, the steps form an equation capable of keeping you on your road to success. Equations are promises that when mathematical relationships are applied to a set of variables, a predictive outcome is expected. Equations can also help solve for the unknown. Your NRID is the key that unlocks and solves for the unknown in the equation for your success.

The NRID system links vital elements of your life into a custom code unique to your wealth identity. Once unlocked, it reveals your path to narrow your road, allowing you to shift gears to indicators unique to you. Once applied to your life, your wealth identity identifies the gaps, allowing you to accelerate your journey to wealth your way. To complete your journey, you must intimately know and apply your NRID to best exchange value with others. Since wealth is a group process, knowing how to be confident in leading, learning, executing, and connecting with others is essential for living a fulfilled life.

Remember that history plays an important part in seeding the pursuit of life's purpose leading to legacy wealth. As beneficiaries of history, we each pull for unique yet shared narratives. Each NarrowRoad journey begins by separating the key elements of your picture into a framework that brings clarity. Your unique way of visioning, thinking, doing, and speaking will become the foundation of your journey. Once you learn your system for success via the base equation, you will have deeper clarity that will ultimately lead to the freedom few find and even fewer pursue.

The NarrowRoad frame represents a macro view of what will hold the collective, as we invite others to pose for the new picture, we are creating on the road together. Understanding your history (both personal and collaborative), specifically, decisions that led to where we are today plays an important role in framing the picture we will be posing for together.

Let's explore the elements that make up every legacy-wealth building equation so The NarrowRoad can work for you. To appreciate and value the wealth identity revealed in your NRID, you must take the steps along The NarrowRoad to understand and own its parts. The NarrowRoad is based on this premise.

The NarrowRoad principles are:

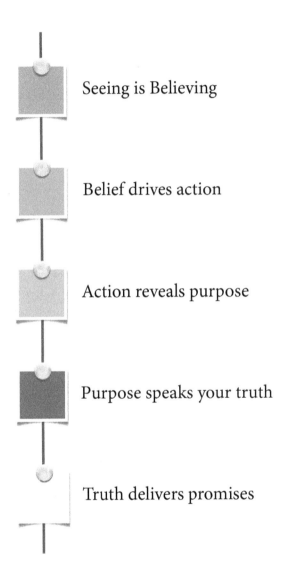

Seeing is Believing

Belief drives action

Action reveals purpose

Purpose speaks your truth

Truth delivers promises

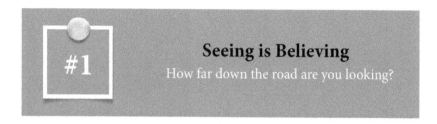

Seeing is Believing
How far down the road are you looking?

NarrowRoad Principle 1—Vision

Vision invites you to invest the time necessary to understand and decode the messages of my grandmother. "The way forward is back through" and "we live what we learn." Hindsight helps identify and clarify vulnerable areas along our road that could lead to blind spots. Looking back on the pitfalls of the past will help lessen our blind spots in the present, where seeing is believing, is meant to focus and clarify our vision. Illuminating just how far down the road we are presently looking and how far we have come.

From this historical perspective, The NarrowRoad explores the depth of vision required to solve for unknowns in its base equation. Beginning with an initial legacy narrative, each journeyer navigates the meta patterns of the previous three generations to clarify their personal legacy perspective. A meta pattern is a pattern of patterns. It can initially look like a maze until you understand how to align the variables, to meet the needs of your wealth equation and make the appropriate choices. Since your first introduction to business is that of your family business, understanding the blueprint you inherited, is key to clarifying the vision for the road ahead. Each generation is asked the question, "Where do we go from here?" To guide you in answering this question, *The NarrowRoad* charts historical financial meta patterns repeated across generations that often require a business understanding of our shared American history. You must also be aware that your theology (the system of your beliefs) is what influences your choices and risk tolerance, inherent in everyone's journey in the pursuit of the most desirable answer to the question. A clear vision is the ability to see how your meta patterns impact a seeing is believing phenomenon; in other words, your vision's unique perspective.

How Far Down the Road Are You Looking—Lifestyle or Legacy

The beauty of a vision, the "aha" moments, is that they come in stages. Like shards of light shining in the right places just at the right time, they give you glimpses and confirm evidence of the possibilities available to you. A vision often emerges in the places where your knowledge has grown dim or never existed. It offers the opportunity you dream of and seems to expand beyond the scope of your experiences and capabilities. Glimpses are those chance moments where you see parts of a whole that have not completely come into plain view. For some, this type of sight is more of a knowing than an actual vision, something almost intuitive.

Throughout my journey, I run into people who often say, "I just know I'm not supposed to end my life in such a negative financial state," or, "this has to stop with me. My children must have a different experience with the financial realities of life."

Financial challenges are prevalent dim spots, but our vision often becomes clearer during a crisis. My research revealed that the financial challenges we face throughout our lives happen at inflection points often recognizable to the older generations but seldom discussed before the next generation can do anything to avoid it. And so, the pattern continues in yet another leg of our history. Some challenges stem from early childhood experiences, some from poor choices made in early adulthood, and others result from a poorly planned retirement. If we let them, inflection points strengthen our faith and serve to narrow our road, to better help clarify our vision on what is required to get out of wandering the financial wilderness.

These experiences are shared by many. How we respond to the glimpses of light is something entirely different. When reminders appear, in an effort to keep the peace of ignorant bliss, some people simply choose to avoid them and run the other way. Others deep dive into the fray, getting lost in dark places, imagining what they saw was more than it was. Others will stand still and wait for the glimpse to reappear. Stepping forward, others invite themselves to peer closer at the light, opening up to learning how to believe in yes. The yes that implies that the time for action is now. The resounding yes, emphasizes it's time to exercise the boldness of our hope.

The first principle of The NarrowRoad, when applied to your unique NRID, reveals your unique ability to see what others cannot yet see and helps to clarify the depth of your perception that becomes the foundation for the next steps beyond the present rocks in your road.

What is your #1 Visionary Role? _____

NarrowRoad Visionary Types	
Quadrant #1	Your #1 Quadrant is how you first SEE the world. Note: Your perspective is your inherited equity. It is the unique lens that shows the way past obstacles and problems. You invest this equity when you share the way you see things every day.
Pure - Visionary	Sees through the lens of wisdom: Your vision is long term, and culturally influenced. You have the wisdom but often not the resources to do all you see.
Thinker - Visionary	Sees through the lens of knowledge: Your vision is near term and relies heavily on an internal need of proof. You need to see first to believe it.
Doer - Visionary	Sees through the lens of experience: Vision for the future is immediate and sparked by activity. Your clarity comes from hands on activity.
Speaker - Visionary	Sees through the lens of expression: Vision for the future is ongoing and sparked by engagement, connection, and feeling.

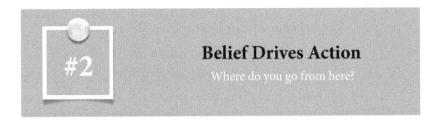

Belief Drives Action

Where do you go from here?

#2

NarrowRoad Principle #2—Thought

Principle two, Thought, is the key to independence and focuses you on declaring your independence.

Wealth at its onset is a strategic, independent pursuit. For this reason, the second principle of The NarrowRoad is concentrated around thought.

Trust and believe that you will find your way of confidently getting to where you want to be. Belief drives action, and a belief system is a strategy to navigate beyond the pitfalls everyone faces when pursuing a promise. Your belief system supports what you know to be true. It guides you to unlock your genius and learn how to pursue your dream.

Along my journey, I wanted to understand if indeed there was this Promised Land of which both the Bible and history speak. If indeed it exists, why then haven't we gotten there? Why does it feel like we're still wandering in the wilderness? I found that there's a pattern to the wilderness. Without a clear strategy in the wilderness, hidden hazards can easily trap the novice, tired, dizzy or frustrated traveler. The distance between an idea of a promise and taking possession of a Promised Land is one of those traps. Do we have the ability to go the distance? Navigating this distance leaves a lot of the journey up to faith because much of the road is largely unseen to the naked eye and untrained anxious mind. Do you have the faith required to navigate the obstacle-riddled road? It is an independent, liberated mind that is willing to go beyond what it currently knows.

Wealth's journey requires a series of decisions that over time build, grow, and expand savings and investments of our talents—we all know this. So why can some people pass wealth from generation to generation, while others seem to remain stuck in the income lane? This is the question I asked of the elders in my study because they'd seen a lot of wandering in the wilderness. I wanted to get their glimpses of the dark places that seem to elude us generationally.

One woman said, "There is no roadmap for the systems that operate around one's life work. Most folks just know how to work with what's in front of them. Pamela, if you want more people to build wealth, well, you're going to have to draw a map for them to see it and then teach them how to believe it." She had built wealth in her lifetime, owning several homes and land that went as far back as her great-grandfather. But unfortunately, because both of her college-educated sons could not find work and lived in her home, she feared they would spend their inheritance while she was alive. Though her wealth would sustain their lifetime, it would not pass on. Even if some were left, neither of her sons were married or had children. No one beyond her offspring would be able to see what she had worked so hard to build. She knew this was a travesty.

Work, and even social life, are a constant stream of decisions. The common element in these decisions is that they are not made in isolation. Income creators often have blind faith in the harvest that will come after the work has been completed. Wealth systems are different from work systems. Wealth creators have unblinded faith that their investments will reap a harvest over time. They invest in the unseen promises of what is to come and have become accustomed to looking for hidden treasure. Thinkers who unlock their genius code with their NRID learn how to believe more because the successful pursuit of their dreams requires it. The most powerful tools for a thinker along The NarrowRoad are the ability to prioritize, taking time to process according to your learning style, and the ability to know the right questions to ask to get the answers you need to succeed.

In a wilderness, you are surrounded by other journeyers whose choices intersect with yours. These individual interactions seem random, but they demonstrate patterns that fund systems and build wealth when looked at from afar.

It was clear on my journey that wealth creators have a financial strategy for their lives that becomes tradition and is passed from generation to generation. Wealth creators learn to value intangible currencies such as cultural, intellectual, and social capital, and use them to access and build even more wealth. This financial strategy is a collective of expertise acquired from the trials and errors of generations before them, who were all in pursuit of a purpose. Over time, the day-to-day management of this wealth-creating strategy is outsourced to people and institutions with even more expertise. The pattern of wealth then becomes a system of growing independence that continues to cross generations.

Those who are skillful creators of wealth for others, such as your banker, financial advisor or investment broker, have a workable strategy for their life that fluctuates with each work situation or job. The difference between creating wealth for others, and being a wealth creator for yourself and family, lies in the awareness of key elements that make up one's wealth identity: your perspective of wealth, your declaration of independence, your ability to manage time, and your willingness to trust your life's pursuit of purpose. It is not all up to you. Wealth creation is a convergence of people, places, and things working together for the good of a promise whose time has come.

Most of these necessary steps are often not yet visible to the new journeyer. Wealth is not just money. An example of a wealth system that does not directly include money is an individual's health system. When one views health as wealth, they have a strategy to maintain good health, including good insurance, regular checkups, and building relationships with doctors you trust. It's taking care of the body that will be the vehicle you will need to pass on wealth to the next generation.

My father, for instance, had two bouts of cancer (June 2013 and May 2014). If not for his history with his chosen physicians, he would not have survived the first bout. Daddy went into remission in late November 2013. His cancer returned with a vengeance the following May. His trust in his doctors and our trust in God made a painful, difficult season bearable. The love demonstrated by the doctors and nurses who had grown accustomed to caring for my father was made possible by the time my father invested with them while he was healthy. My father passed away in late June 2014 in the company of friends and family, which included his team of physicians. Investing the time to preserve his health via his relationship with his doctors, they prescribed the best early treatment, which extended our time with my father. There are wealth systems and work systems—money is nothing but time spent. Death is a gift in the lessons it gives those left behind to continue the legacy.

Awareness of the difference can teach, or at least encourage, people to better strategize on how they spend their finite time incorporating wealth systems into their work systems. Maximizing strategies for wealth and income potential, including the present and the future, is a faster way to get out of the wilderness. A great plan offers a strategic advantage that can be passed on for generations. The second step in your NRID reveals how you best process information and optimizes a strategy for financial independence.

What is your #2 Thought Role? _____

NarrowRoad Thinker Types		
Quadrant #2	**Your #2 Quadrant is how you THINK.** Note: Your second role is the way you process information, grow, evaluate ideas and build confidence. This is the key that unlocks your genius code as you pursue independence.	
Visionary - Thinker	Thought process is based on independent observations. You often need to take a step back and see the bigger picture to increase confidence.	☐
Pure - Thinker	Thought process is based on learning and thinking things through independently. You often require additional time alone to reach a level of confidence about an opportunity.	☐
Doer - Thinker	Thought process is based on independent activity. You often figure things out by spending time doing it on your own and or "working it through with your hands."	☐
Speaker - Thinker	Thought process is based on engagement and inquiry. You often can translate what others are thinking into a language most can understand.	☐

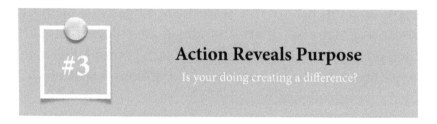

Action Reveals Purpose

Is your doing creating a difference?

#3

NarrowRoad Principle #3—Action

The third step of The NarrowRoad is action. Action is essential to your pursuit of legacy wealth. Consistent doing makes the difference between a dream of wealth and a mission to create it. The Israelites' initial exodus deposited them into the wilderness on the way to the Promised Land. There were specific things they had to do to take full possession of the promise. In the wilderness, each member of each tribe had a job to do. The tribes operated under one of four standards: lion, man, ox, eagle. When the silver trumpet blew, everyone knew that their mission was to move further down the road to another part of the wilderness.

When it comes to action, the four standards represented a sequence of timed execution. The Levites, a tribe, tasked with remaining in the center of the wilderness surrounded by the four standards, had to lead the way to exit the wilderness. The standard on the east side of the centermost camp was the first after those charged with leading everyone, followed by the southern standard, the western standard, and the northern. Knowing when to pursue your promise is just as important as choosing to pursue it. There is a time and a season for everything. Everyone has a window of time. Managing your time ensures you maximize your window. In their unique way, everyone is doing something to create wealth for themselves by working with a standard of living.

Along The NarrowRoad, you will learn that if one can create wealth for others, they can create it for themselves. It's all in the way your talents and abilities are valued. Have you taken the time to calculate a personal level of enough? Take some time now to ask the wealth builder in you: How much wealth is enough? You may ask, enough of what? Enough resources (human, social, intellectual, cultural, and spiritual) to build wealth your way. Wealth creation is really up to you and how you define it. I have found we all have more than we think we do. As a result, we are all working with more than we think. Your time (as an example) is extremely important in calculating enough. For some in the Promised Land narrative, wandering in the wilderness for 40 years was enough. For others, it was about going further down the road to take possession of the inherited promise. What is enough for you? Once you have found your answer, then ask, "What are you doing to reach your *enough*?"

Your life along The NarrowRoad is the owner of a portfolio of assets. Your journey through life occurs during a timed window of opportunity. Capacity, commitment, and persistence are necessary elements of a fruitful journey. There may be various harvests you can reap. However, they are not what will get you to the position of enough. A position of enough requires knowing the true cost of what you desire, so you can be the best steward of your portfolio of assets to take possession of your desires. Within the window called your career, getting to enough is beyond the circular pattern of getting up and going to work for 40 years to sustain the lifestyle you desire post-retirement. Some people work their entire lives toward the expected harvest of retirement, only to find they don't have the capacity or the resources to enjoy life as they'd hoped. The lesson here is that budgeting for the long term will get you further down the road in the lifestyle of your choice rather than hoping all will be ok; that is an example of blind faith. Your thought pattern formed in the wilderness raises the awareness of what is needed to create an action pattern. Your action pattern is the way you do things to create with the assets you have, to accumulate the resources needed for enough and beyond.

A NarrowRoad principle is action reveals purpose. It is our human capital that will build our life portfolio. It is blood, sweat, and tears that will create the life desired. Developing talents that create specific ways to multiply your talents get you past enough to the life passionately desired. Belief drives action. Action drives creativity. Creativity ignites income creation. Income creation drives wealth creation. What do you do best? Owning it is a requirement to build wealth your way.

My research confirmed the saying, "whatever you believe you can do is exactly what you can do." We've all heard the adage that time is money. Time is not just money; it is so much more. Everything takes time to create—from a rewarding career to the fulfillment of a promise. The extent to which you believe in your abilities is not exclusive of what you are capable of, but it does carry the highest probability of what you will attempt. While this enables one to have various successful experiences, it leaves many resources untapped and underdeveloped. Untapped and underdeveloped resources, with a little (unblind) faith, can finance your pursuit of legacy wealth. When applied to your unique NRID, the third principle reveals the talent most useful for your income-earning pursuit.

What is your #3 Action Role? _____

NarrowRoad Doer Types

Quadrant #3	Your #3 Quadrant is your PRIMARY ASSET Note: Your third role the easiest element of your identity to MONETIZE and the key talent you are recognized for	☑
Visionary - Doer	Your strength is driven by your ability to see the end goal and focus the efforts of others to attain it. You align the end with the beginning. With insight you develop moving parts into a model that works.	
Thinker - Doer	Your strength is driven by your ability to use your knowledge to identify improve the current situation. You consult with others to understand those who desire to know how to improve. With the right information you make things better.	
Pure - Doer	Your strength is driven by your ability to complete the necessary steps to create momentum. With the right to-do list you get things done.	
Speaker - Doer	Your strength is driven by your ability to intuit the needs of the current situation and speak in a way that motivates and encourages others. Your words encourage, direct and guide way forward. With the right message you move mountains.	

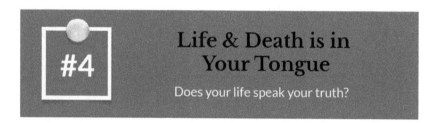

The NarrowRoad Principle #4—Speech

The fourth step along The NarrowRoad is Speech. This principle is focused on the importance of finding your voice, defining your message and using both your voice and your message to build your freedom in a Promised Land. The Israelites escaped Egyptian slavery, transitioning to a wilderness period that was not slavery. By their design (fear of the unknown), they were not entirely free. Within freedom is an understanding that to stay there, one must be willing to work, save, and invest in maintaining the standard of life desired. To continue to afford to keep operating, one must find their voice, ask for what they want, and respond to the invitations to assist in getting there.

Your voice expresses what you feel. It is the energy that keeps the promise alive and capable of transferring across generations. Your speech is what builds the energy required for a collective pursuit of a desired degree of freedom. Speech is how you use your voice along The NarrowRoad. It's what invites others to collaborate with you along your journey. It is, in many ways, why people connect with you. Yet many consciously or unconsciously remain silent, stuck between the various stages of the pursuit toward the Promised Land, waiting for the right time and right way to speak their truth.

Why is this so? Is it due to fear of rejection, fear of acceptance, or a lack of clarity defining the truth? Or, is it a fear of success and what that may mean for friends and family who choose to disconnect from you? Is it a need to define the keywords that determine the level of wealth one desires to create; words such as lifetime value, middle-class, and legacy? How does one define freedom so others will understand and want to subscribe? What is a democracy, and how does your voice contribute to it? Becoming more conscious of answers to these collective questions is how to unmute. It is how we find our voices and build a standard that supports our desired degree of freedom for our business, our immediate and extended family and our broader community businesses.

In our unique way, we all speak differently while often saying the same words. Our voices don't all sound the same, nor do they come from the same place. Step number four is about finding the origin of our voice—the who, what, and where of how it was influenced. Owning your voice is a two-step process along The NarrowRoad; finding it and using it.

The creation of the U.S. Constitution, the outcomes the Israelites faced on the final leg of their journey to the Promised Land, and the undesirable yet unsilenced voice of Dr. Martin Luther King Jr., seeking unity and justice for America, are examples of the importance of building a life system that speaks your truth in ways that pass on for generations. How does one go about building a voice that speaks beyond the moment to leave a lasting legacy message?

Silence is present during our childhood. In previous generations, the mantra was, 'kids are to be seen and not heard.' If you are the kids of those generations, you learned to be mute early. Children don't have the ability or skills to sort through life's complicated events and end up burying emotions and attaching specific judgments to those feelings. The simple event of being laughed at on the first day of school or as detrimental as witnessing the death of a loved one leave indelible marks. As kids, our ideas of the world and where we fit into it are still developing—yet when a defining moment arises, it scores marks on the worksheet of who we are in a painful way. This pain, which is unique to each of us, lies in the shadows of our being. Unable to sort through this childhood pain or disappointment forces us (as adults) to make decisions to avoid that same feeling or memory. It's often difficult to revisit our childhood. In order to heal, we must unpack the wound to release our voice.

If you are unhappy with our world today, my question to you is, "What truth is your life speaking?" When applied to your unique NRID, the fourth principle reveals just how to start unmuting to secure the solutions you need. Unmuting your voice breaks the pattern of repeated mistakes of the past. It is one of the most important steps along The NarrowRoad.

What is your #4 Speaker role? _____

NarrowRoad Speaker Types

Quadrant #4	Your #4 Quadrant is how you SPEAK, or send messages. Note: Your fourth role is your weakest and most underdeveloped role in your inventory of treasure. This is the key that once matured will be your greatest resource of strength and freedom.	☐
Visionary - Speaker	Your eyes tell the real story; you have the ability to see through words, and expressions of others when in the group. Your emotions often impact your ability to see clearly.	
Thinker - Speaker	Your mind speaks your real truth; you can synthesize the opinions of other groups. Your emotions often impact your ability to make decisions.	
Doer - Speaker	Your actions speak louder than your words, and you prefer group collaboration to get things done. Your emotions impact your ability to do things consistently.	
Pure - Speaker	Your words speak the real truth; you have the ability to say what everyone else is really feeling. Your emotions impact how much you share and with who.	

My NarrowRoad journey began with the affirmation of what I do best. For as long as I can remember, speaking was the gift that made room for me. I would talk to my great grandparents as a little child, and I remember their eyes would light up when they listened to me. My father, mother, and brother would listen and tell me people needed to hear my voice. Classmates at Wharton would pull me aside and say, "You have a gift. When you speak, people want to do something." I used this talent to sell car stereo equipment at Circuit City to pay for college. In my role as a banker, I used this talent to sell the hardest product out there; money. I used this talent to collect terabytes of data from people to create The NarrowRoad. I use this talent to motivate people across the country around their unique abilities to build legacy wealth. I use this talent to synthesize research about black wealth for my clients and my community.

My appreciation of this talent remained buried for years. I only valued it when others told me it was valuable. My focus stayed on what I could not do at the level of my peers (my weakest quadrant Q4). This is what hampered my confidence (quadrant 2) and kept me wandering in the financial wilderness.

I kept exploring how to see my way to success by thinking and learning in classrooms (my strongest quadrant 1).

Every time I let my talents make room for me, amazing things happen. While on a panel in Atlanta, a representative from a large bank heard me answer a question from a woman concerned about the progress of our community. Duly impressed with my answer, she sponsored me to speak at the bank's events across the country. Executives and leaders would hear me speak at these events and hire me to speak to their employees and serve as a strategist for their companies. Believers would hear me speak and invite me to meet their pastors, priests, and rabbis, who invited me to preach and teach to their congregations. Parents and teachers would hear me speak and invite me to speak to their schools and children. While this was great, I would still focus on what I could not do in Q4. I felt that there was more for me to do, and my inability to ask for the help I needed made me feel stuck and incapable of adding the real value I desired. Unmuting begins when you face any and all fears concerning your weaknesses in your 4th quadrant. We all have a message to share. Understanding how your life speaks its truth is the beginning of building a life that connects to what it needs to succeed.

Truth Delivers Outcomes

Is your best further down the road?

#5

The NarrowRoad Principle #5—Outcome

The fifth principle along The NarrowRoad is Outcome. Truth delivers on promises in the form of a definitive outcome. This principle is concentrated on the importance of anchoring your journey to a series of milestones and metrics that keep you focused on continuing to progress further down the road; beyond survival, beyond freedom, toward growth and expansion. The fifth step of The NarrowRoad supports the belief that legacy wealth is anchored to a multigenerational pursuit of a definable outcome that starts with a seed and builds and grows over time. Your first desired outcome will be based on elements from the prior four principles and influenced by those in the family line who journeyed ahead of you. These add up to a series of legacy metrics that are further defined by financial milestones. The ultimate desired outcome to be achieved throughout your lifetime is the continued execution of your legacy wealth blueprint. A written vision with four defined milestones leads further down the road toward what you can achieve given your current situation.

- Milestone One is to create a life of increasing levels of income.
- Milestone Two is to build a sustainable lifestyle that extends beyond retirement.

- Milestone Three is to enculturate wealth by increasing ownership and investment in things that matter to you and future generations.
- Milestone Four is to ensure the legacy of your wealth expands beyond you to future generations, leaving this world better than you found it.

I have found that the road to wealth is paved with good intentions. Many dreamers are sincere about becoming and remaining wealth creators. Of those dreamers, many create a financial plan. Some consult with a financial advisor, and others have an idea for how their life will financially play out. What is lacking in the dream is accountability and consistency to keep the best intentions focused on the promise ahead. Choosing to remain committed to your NarrowRoad principles for legacy wealth is how you ensure that your vision for wealth becomes a reality.

Blind spots along the road include a lack of accountability to yourself and others. The lack of acceptable measurement methods to create and build wealth. The lack of follow-through in personal financial performance to grow wealth your way. The lack of successful models of pursuits of legacy wealth to ensure all that you have won is not lost after you are gone. Leaving the steps of creating, building, growing, and expanding wealth unfinished renders the "how-to" a hidden secret kept from the very people in your wealth group who need to hear, learn, see, and follow your lead to attain it. The wandering in the financial wilderness will continue. This is why generation after generation in communities born into inherited promises have to start over from the beginning again and again.

This fifth principle along The NarrowRoad enables everyone who desires to get to the promise of legacy wealth the accountability of the vision whose time has finally come. Desired outcomes show clearly what together you as a family, or group, can do in this lifetime and beyond. Desired outcomes can be passed on for generations and can be shared across friends and families. Think of desired outcomes as inherited opportunities that took generations to be delivered, at just the right time, in just the right place. Your desired outcomes begin as something personal to you and end as a glimpse of light in the dark places we all face while in the financial wilderness. Your desired outcome, once achieved, becomes a model others can study and follow if they choose. This is how step number five expands the legacy wealth narrative in a language you understand. Charting your path in this way becomes something worthwhile for you and for others who want to believe as you do but need that glimpse of light called you.

What is your desired outcome? _____

The NarrowRoad Outcomes		
Quadrant #5	Your 5th Quadrant contains the desired outcomes at the end of each bend in the NarrowRoad. Note: Your fitfh quadrant is what shadows your progress along your jouney. It becomes your anchor that does not change until you have attained your desired outcome.	☑
Legacy Outcome	Long-Term Outcome: To pass on wealth to the next generation. (However you define it.)	
Growth Outcome	Near-Term: To grow beyond living a lifestyle to the pursuit of financial independence by owning the business of you.	
Mission Outcome	Immediate: To create a realistic budget, move beyond survival and consistently multiply your talents to attain a degree of freedom that satisfies your wants and needs.	
Purpose Outcome	Ongoing: To build and pursue a standard of wealth for myself and share the journey with others I care about.	

The NarrowRoad is a guide for the perplexed. It is a guide for those who are tired of knowing they could be more, live fuller lives, yet have trouble clarifying the what, how, where, and why to be "free at last." Once the perplexed create their NarrowRoad map, the day of overcoming has arrived. Your journey helps you clarify the road that lies ahead. Your personalized roadmap helps you see your way from an idea to a dream and on to a mission and purpose of the promise for which you have been waiting. Once clear on your mission and purpose, you will progress further along the road of pursuit to the promise as designed by you.

True freedom happens when you own your path to promise and take the leap of unblinded faith to get there. If you recall the Bible verse in Matthew from which The NarrowRoad is named; "Enter through the narrow gate. For wide is the gate, and broad is the road that leads to destruction, and many enter through it. But small is the gate and narrow the road that leads to life, and only a few find it." Take the leap of faith. Your choices narrow the road. The only risk is when you stay stuck amongst your options.

My grandfather Alphonse Jolly said to me, "Baby girl, in life, there are many options but only one choice that is right for you—choose wisely." He also said, "Never be an options girl; only be a choice girl when dating men." But that's a story for another guide along The NarrowRoad.

Life is filled with choices. You can do what you want and be who you desire by focusing on the road ahead and being willing to learn from many teachers along the way. Your promise can be within reach. Choose things in sequences that lead to your promised success and then boldly live the life you were promised. That is the belief embedded in The NarrowRoad that unblinds your faith. What you will find as you journey along The NarrowRoad is that you have a jumpstart—parts of your road's vision have already been "made plain." For you to see it, just connect the parts to your roadmap to one that charts a path to wealth. Enjoy this discovery phase of your journey! If you'd like to navigate your roadmap with fellow wealth-building friends or need assistance, navigate your way to: *www.mynarrowroad.com/roadmap* and let's begin your path to making your journey along The NarrowRoad come into plain sight.

Anchoring to Outcomes Along The NarrowRoad

Key Elements of The NarrowRoad Equation

The following questions help you better understand The Narrow-Road you're traveling. Answer as honestly as you can. If you're honest with yourself, your road will narrow to a path conducive to your success. There are no right or wrong answers, even if they don't match everything you've read in this book. For legacy wealth to be attainable, it must be defined by you and the choices you understand and commit to making.

Principle 1: Seeing is believing. Describe your first role (how you see): I see with my... (hands, eyes, mind, mouth)

_____

_____

Principle 2: Belief drives action. Describe your second role (how you think): I think with my...(hands, eyes, mind, mouth)

_____

_____

Principle 3: Action reveals purpose. Describe your third role (how you do): I best operate with my...(hands, eyes, mind, mouth)

_____

_____

Principle 4: Purpose speaks your truth. Describe your fourth role (how you speak): I communicate my truth with my...(hands, eyes, mind, mouth)

_____

_____

Principle 5: Truth delivers promises. Describe the desired outcome you have concerning wealth you want to pursue in your lifetime (what you will promise yourself to finish in your lifetime). I will navigate the road to wealth beyond (survival, comfort, independence) to a financial legacy that passes on for generations.

_____

_____

Principle 6: Considering the options above, describe a desired outcome you have concerning wealth you want to pursue in your lifetime:

_____

_____

Your NarrowRoad Equation

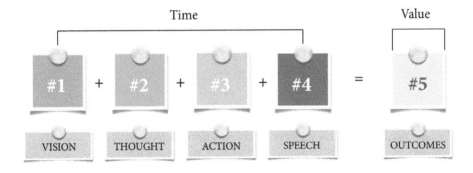

How to create, build, grow, and expand wealth along your NarrowRoad journey is unique to your NRID. This is how you build wealth for yourself. "Wealth your way".

Chapter Three

RULES OF THE ROAD

The method used to build this roadmap is a narrative survey. It consists of a series of questions, when answered and reflected upon through the lens of your NRID, begins a journey. The journey from where you presently are in the wilderness to the next desired degree of freedom.

- Entry gate—Finding my NarrowRoad ID.
- Assessment—Where am I in the wilderness?
- Wealth checklist—Where are the blind spots along my road?
- Inquiry—What is my strategy to define and own where I want to go from here?
- Convincing—What must I do (now, next, ongoing, long-term)?
- Persuasion—What must I ask for from my wealth team and demand of myself?
- Negotiation—How far down the road must I look to get where I desire to travel?
- What must I face and change to get beyond my roadblock?

Your life is what you make of it. You are a servant with the potential of five talents capable of planting seeds and reaping harvests. Your life is yours to design how you see fit. Life is truly a gift when viewed this way. Regardless of where you begin, where you end is entirely up to you and the choices you make along the road. The road is the same for everyone.

The NarrowRoad method outlines the options available to you. A few clear choices help you detail what you desire to build, grow, expand, and finally arrive at your ultimate desired outcome. Your choices, in turn, customize The NarrowRoad journey beginning from where you currently are positioned in the financial wilderness to where you desire to go. These choices offered are the requirements to get you there.

Perspective is shaped by your history, your experiences, your confidence, and your vulnerabilities. Where have you come from as an individual? As a member of society? As a leader of your pursuit of promise? How far back down the road have you looked? What is the history you have already created? Writing your story leads to writing your vision as a narrative connected to those who have come before you. Making a plan with the assistance of your NRID is how you go deeper. Waiting for it is how you operate the business of you. Seeing it come to pass is how you actualize your legacy.

Financial growth is really about strategizing toward the level of financial independence you believe is right for you. Each level has fundamental steps needed to grow your desired level of independence. For example, the level of financial independence you desire post-retirement narrows the road to a few select strategies in which to save and invest. College financial planning for your children is similar. Learn the fundamentals, and your strategy for financial independence takes shape.

Strategy is at the root of your confidence. The use of applied knowledge helps you weather any storm in your life, a downturn in the market, and disappointment in your point of view. Are you confident you are pursuing wealth with the right strategy?

Consistency is the key to fruitful outcomes. Anything will work if you work it; anything. I used to buy all of this workout equipment and would soon grow tired of it, and I would tell anyone who would listen that the equipment simply did not work. My trainer would say, "If you worked it, it would work just as promised. You gave up—it didn't." Consistency is key to moving further down the road, closer to the authentic you. Where are you most consistent in your life? Where are you the least consistent? Why? Belief drives action. The NarrowRoad roadmap will work if you work it. Your NarrowRoad ID will tell us what needs to be reinforced in your strategy. Consistency is a choice to which you commit. To arrive at a state of consistency requires looking at your beliefs in the areas your consistency needs assistance. Wealth is a group process; we all need support to succeed.

Maturity is how we get where we desire to go. Our relationship with money can be very emotional. It is time to face our deepest fears about the desires of our hearts. Life is a scary place when you avoid facing what matters most. You find yourself alone, faking it till you make it. How mature are your emotions? In matters of the heart and wealth, one must play to their strengths and weaknesses to build their desired life. When it comes to what you desire most, how mature are you really? What must you face to get beyond where you are most comfortable? There is always 'more' further down the road to wealth as a legacy.

Accountability is who holds you accountable for your ideas and dreams inherent in your perspective? Remaining consistent, staying true to your strategy, and getting mature all require accountability. As we get older, accountability partners are not optional—you'll find they need to be a staple in your life-purpose pursuit. An accountability network is key.

Our Journey

The NarrowRoad Degree of Freedom

Time & Chance
happen to us all

To every thing there is a
season, and a time to
every purpose under
the heaven.

— Ecclesiastes 3:1

Influence

Independence

Class

Income

"You can only see as far you can afford."
—Vincent Jolly Sr.

| Human Capital | Social Capital | Intellectual Capital | Cultiral Capital | Spiritual Capital |

Armed with the above requirements of the road, many of us still need a roadmap to see the road we are on to determine if it's the best road to take. It starts with anchoring the end of your current situation to an outcome. For every generation, roadmaps have existed to assist the collective pursuit of purpose—roadmaps such as the Bible, the longest-reigning guideline still available for identifying and pursuing life's purpose. Other tools such as Stephen R. Covey's *The 7 Habits of Highly Effective People*, Carl Jung-inspired Myers-Briggs Personality Test, astrology, numerology, and religion, have updated the cannon for our times. They all suggest that we must fully appreciate who we are as the first step of our journey.

Our NarrowRoad roadmap is the blueprint for how you will get it done. The journey to wealth is how you will apply the concepts learned about your unique identity to your possession of promise. In Part One, we learned that history is prophecy if you connect the dots of wisdom, knowledge and understanding. The journey to wealth along The NarrowRoad has four steps that occur individually and collectively at the same time. It occurs individually along the journey as you pursue each step your way. It also occurs collectively as a continuation of a legacy narrative that did not start with you and will not end with you, unless you discontinue the conversation. Your journey is a dialog with your past, present and future that turns the generational wheel of wealth forward.

Picking up the torch is a unique opportunity everyone can consider along their life's journey. While it may not seem like it, it's far easier to build on something already existing than to start from scratch. Building from scratch may appear to deliver quicker results in the short term, but it does not. Long-term, avoiding the obstacle-filled path already overcome by others leads means reaching the same position and going farther down the road at an accelerated pace. Consider connecting the dots of your legacy, the 80% already known, to inform and establish the roadmap uniquely available to you. Building already existing systems from scratch is ultimately what will be the very thing that will slow down the journey toward a new venture—which just happens to be further down the road on which you are traveling but cannot yet see. This is a true statement both for life and business. Life, similar to business, is 80 percent the same and only 20 percent different. The 20 percent is your perspective, while the 80 percent is standard operating procedures common to all lives and businesses. The questions to ask yourself at this point: Is the vision you have for your life based on a solid idea? Have you taken the time to enlighten yourself about the value of the paths that have come before you? Am I trying to reinvent the wheel? If 80% of the roadmap is the same for everyone, then focus on the 20% that is uniquely yours and remember the first rule of the road is: The Way Forward is Really Back Through.

As we entered the gate to The NarrowRoad, we began looking back at what came before us to help inform our journey of the 80% completed roadmap. As this biblical scripture and common day adage (found in Ecclesiastes 9:11) states, there is nothing new under the sun. Time and chance happen to all. Your time and chances improve significantly if time is taken to anchor the steps of the journey to a destination beyond prior pursuits. What you ultimately desire to do will begin with greater equity when you take the time to pick up a torch. A torch is an unfulfilled dream of someone before you—it is unfinished business waiting for you and your inherited opportunities to pursue; a torch-bearer. It can be someone famous or someone special to you. In my case, I shine a light on my ancestors. As an African-American, I am particularly interested in the missing narrative of my people as you should be in yours.

By choice or by force, America is a nation of immigrants. Regardless of ethnicity or nationality, your families decided to or were forced to migrate to a new country to build, earn, learn, and expand on what they could not achieve in their own lands. The skills they brought with them were what was needed in this country, and build it they did. Regardless of how we got here, we all became Americans. The harvest was not equally shared for Americans in general, but specifically African-Americans. The height of the Civil Rights movement was a time of exodus into a wilderness for not only them but also for our nation. It was a time that prepared many for the great battles that stood between a willingness to fight, the necessity to fight, and the collective action of equitable sharing of the harvest that is necessary to take full possession of the Promised Land.

Ownership is a responsibility. Oversights can occur without a strategy that looks beyond paying the mortgage to the reward of taking full possession of the land by all who labored to build it. Oversight, blind spots or intentional omission can cause the Promise to slip between the gaps across generations. The legacy perspective gets lost in translation if not connected to a larger community narrative and understanding of the impact of decisions.

In post-emancipation America, the split in the roads taken beyond emancipation defined the various degrees of freedom in every community today. Instead of sharing the bounty reaped from the labor of Africans, greed and hatred led to America's most heinous history. A forced assimilation and acculturation of others who feared that the oversights would affect them adversely.

Within the American narrative, African-Americans share a distance of approximately 150 years from slavery. This interrupted much of the connection to their ancestral roots, and therefore, their narrative. Amid this shared distance of 150 years, they too had a choice of four roads along their journey: rocky, thorny, filled with landmines, or fertile. Their truncated history would greatly influence their journey. Yet the African-American legacy narrative contains one of the most valuable business lessons for anyone desiring to pursue financial independence to pass on for generations. Standing in financial equality is one of the keys to African-American "freedom."

With a truncated history, often, our first inflection point in our lives is our emancipation at eighteen. How we extend the legacy of what our parents and grandparents invested in us is our legacy pursuit of freedom and equality. Looking past the financial emancipation of our first eighteen to twenty years, and how you pick up and carry the torch, in what I call building the family business. Our emancipation then requires that we must be connected to our genesis, as the past teaches repeatedly, the core elements of what must be used to build an independent and free life for oneself.

The African-American community has a multitude of business lessons inherent in their history because of their shared inherited legacy narrative. African-Americans are the only segment of the American population who were first capital before they made capital. Their ancestral roots are just not a matter of memory, history, legacy, and tradition; they are a matter of public financial records. Africans came to America on the balance sheets of emergent plantation business owners desiring to build a better life for their families by any means necessary. Within this pursuit was the use of slavery as a business model. Besides the land, the enslaved Africans carried the most value on the financial statement of early America. They were the human assets whose work created the products America used to build tremendous wealth in one of the shortest periods in history. A legacy that began as extreme creators of wealth for others. To reconcile our country means the way forward is looking back, understanding, and appreciating the roles played by each tribe to build this great nation.

Today many African-Americans are figuratively and literally journeying back to the land of their origin to get a glimpse of a history they will never fully understand. Still, a glimpse may be enough to fully recognize their value and right to attain equality in their inherited homeland. Standing in financial equality is one of the keys to African-American "freedom" and is an indication that America is ready to take full possession of its Promise.

Chapter Four

PORTFOLIO OF TALENTS

What happens to a dream deferred?
Does it dry up
like a raisin in the sun?
Or fester like a sore—
And then run?
Does it stink like rotten meat?
Or crust and sugar over—
like a syrupy sweet?
Maybe it just sags
like a heavy load.
Or does it explode?

— **Langston Hughes,** "A Dream Deferred"

What Is Your Dream?

We all have dreams. Snapshots of a future that, with just a little faith, will come to fruition. What is your dream? Have you ever taken the time to figure out the cost?

Cost means more than just money. Think through what it will take to attain it in terms of *time, talent and treasure*? All dreams require the investment of these three elements. Every dream, in some way, is financed with people's time, spent leveraging people's talent to acquire the desired treasure.

I have learned a dream will only get you so far down the road. There is more to the journey than coming up with an idea and dreaming it as possible. Some dreams take generations to come to fruition; some can appear to happen instantly. A dream fulfilled brings wealth to all who took the time to believe in it. In this instance, wealth is the ability to bear fruit in places some never knew existed. The faith part of a dream is belief in something beyond yourself. While it's true that 78 percent of America associates themselves with some form of Christian faith tradition, beyond fact, my research revealed that just about everyone, when faced with a financial challenge or confusing situation, simply closes their eyes and prays...because they believe in something. A dream of the future has within in it both faith and finance.

In your hands rests the wealth-navigation tool committed to meeting you where you are and guiding you however far down the road of wealth you desire to travel.

"Through understanding, it is established." Proverbs 24:3

To erect a house, you must build walls. Walls are the decisions, choices and actions you must make along the road to wealth. They govern your roadmap and help design your pursuit out of the financial wilderness. Knowledge is different from education. Education is what you buy; knowledge is what you own. Knowledge is education applied to confidence, leading to a level of acumen. This is the type of knowledge required for executing decisions focused on taking possession of the promise of legacy wealth in your life. You already know that history and your personal history can become prophecy when viewed in this way.

Everyone Is Born With a Portfolio of Talents

Your Portfolio of Talents

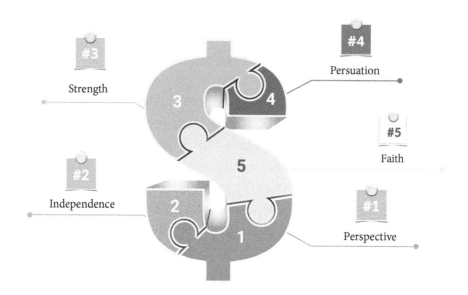

Like capital, talent comes in various forms, such as your ability to manage time, connect and exchange with others, partner with opportunities worth pursuing, and align with perspectives not your own. Invested capital is equity, and when one has equity, one has shares of ownership of something valuable. When one decides to pursue legacy wealth, there are stores of treasure hidden within you that you have not yet seen. Treasure that is buried in the core of who you are. Your purpose is to uncover the true messages of why you are here and what you have to share with the world. That is where the wealth that passes on for generations is stored. Every seed that reaches the fertile ground is promised to reap a harvest. Some of us are blessed enough to arrive at inflection points in life when we take a moment to be introspective. To say, "My life is amazing, it's fun, relevant, and

I believe I'm making a difference." That is a powerful statement that leads to even more miraculous outcomes. On your journey, if you arrive at a point where you feel you could continue on this road for the rest of your life, this is when the road has narrowed to your point of life's purpose. Your life has spoken your truth, and your heart has found its desires and is at peace.

The messages you heard and followed along your journey are like systems: they integrate ideas, dreams, missions, and promises into cooperative exchanges people can feel and believe. Your life speaks its truest purpose when the innermost desires of your heart are on a path to the fulfillment of your truth—you are wealth. When what you desire most for yourself, your community, our world, and your legacy find purpose, you cannot help but produce more wealth.

A fulfilled life requires big changes to open your eyes to what is further down the road. Focusing on the now is not only easy, but it's also comfortable. For most, thoughts about the future are left up to faith, hope, and a dream. In the beginning, the road to clarity is still very wide. It is filled with options that could lead to a life you desire or not. A strategy is needed to narrow the road and focus your attention on finding the optimum direction for your path. These big changes only happen when people can afford to see that change is necessary. Only when our vision and understanding shift perspective further down the road can the business of our lives reflect our hopes and dreams. The financial implications of these moves propel us forward and are the driving forces that impact the business of you and that of your community.

The Talents in Your Portfolio

Your ability to see, think, do, speak, and arrive at outcomes is unique to your portfolio of talents. Each of us speaks, thinks, and arrives at our outcomes based on our historical perspective. Learning to maximize our best talents means cultivating connections between wisdom, knowledge, and understanding, the keys to successfully navigating beyond various options as we journey toward building a wealth portfolio with our financial capacity.

Two Bible verses set the context for the *raison d'être* of The NarrowRoad:

Proverbs 2:6: "For the LORD giveth wisdom: out of his mouth cometh knowledge and understanding." (King James Version).

Proverbs 24:4: "By wisdom, a house is built, and through understanding, it is established; through knowledge, its rooms are filled with rare and beautiful treasures." (New International Version).

A key first step in building wealth is getting your financial house in order. How you accomplish this is through the wisdom of those who came before. Your introduction to business occurred in your childhood, where you were taught what to do and also what not to do with money to pursue wealth. It was here that your financial house and life foundation were established. How did you grow up with money, value, leadership, and confidence? My research showed that two generations ago when our grandparents were seeding, building, growing and expanding the world as we know it today, many of them found it necessary to believe that "one day" God would make it all okay and that we would all overcome. When you go back four generations (if you can), all they had was God to put their minds at ease. The way you grew up with money, values, leadership, confidence and otherwise, is a continuation of those faith-filled beliefs.

By wisdom, a house is built.

From the foundation of wisdom, you choose how to create your own financial house. Your current financial situation reveals how much wisdom lies in the foundation of your house. Establishing a financial house requires using all five capitals in your toolkit: human, social, intellectual, cultural and spiritual. The more wisdom you deploy, the more capital you allocate toward creating the assets you need to establish yourself. Cracks in your foundational wisdom show up as inconsistencies in your understanding of how wealth is created. Cracks show up in the form of:

>**Chaos**—where you work hard and die trying.

>**Isolation**—where you go it alone and fake it until you hopefully make it.

>**Confusion**—where your insecurities block you from learning and applying what you need to succeed.

>**Blindness**—where your blind spots threaten your vision whose time has finally come.

The jolly good news is that this is not a permanent problem. It's just a current situation that your NRID will help you get beyond. From this foundation of wisdom, you will choose how to create your financial pursuit. Knowledge of self is what's required to exit the financial wilderness. Taking the time to know who you are, what you desire for your life, assess how best to pursue those desires, and ask for help when needed, is how you grow the confidence required to believe in your dreams. Taking responsibility for your mission once you've chosen to accept it is the next step.

Chapter Five

CAPITAL ALONG THE NARROWROAD: THE BUSINESS OF YOU

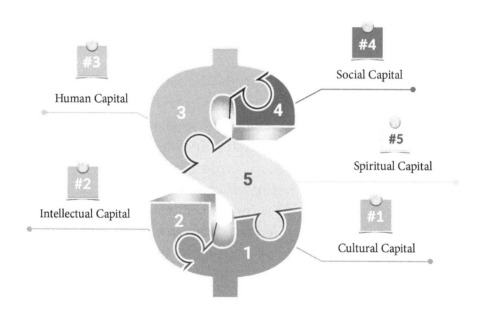

These 5 capitals are your portfolio of assets.
Each capital is within your control to fuel your pursuit
of life, liberty, & promise.

There are five forms of capital along The NarrowRoad—human, social, intellectual, cultural, and spiritual; they make up your portfolio of assets. Armed and confident of these five assets, you have everything you need to fund your pursuit of the promise. There's a belief that we have a capital issue in our society. That's simply not true. At best, we have an allocation issue. At worst, we have a connection and a trust issue. With what you've been blessed with, you can do what you are called to do to forge a bridge in the gaps noted. Our ancestor's legacy narratives prove this.

To gain an understanding of this, let's talk about the business of you. Everyone with a financial statement is in business. What is different between your business and any other is your perspective and how your unique view influences the way you operate. Like any business, the business of you uses capital to build, grow, and expand. The business of you is largely the same as everyone else's. It has a product, a market, an opportunity cost, a price, and your intangible ingenuity; time-sixty minutes in an hour, twenty-four hours a day, and seven days a week is what's allotted for building.

A business remains in business by creating and selling a product. What is your product or talent multiplier? What capital do you use to create your product? How is it delivered? Why is it valuable? Who determines the value? How do you make money? Everyone in business must answer the what, how, why, and who questions about their operating model. Anyone with a financial statement is in business; anyone. Those who took the time and spent the money to incorporate are entrepreneurs, and those who work for someone else every day are intrapreneurs. The business is largely the same; it's just the perspectives that are different. To be clear, every one of us is in business to some extent. I ask again, do you own it?

The operating model to run a business can be complex. Operations determine how the business should be done, why it should be done that way, and who is in control of making sure it gets done.

Once Moses died, it seems the operating system for the Israelites changed. A new vision and new thought leadership arose. What I believe sparked the change in the wilderness wandering plan was the desire to be something more than a people who had escaped Egyptian slavery, and though at break-even, albeit blessed, they desired to create and build something of their own. That decision required two things: the courage to fight for the collective dream and the determination to engage in your part of the operating system that makes the promise viable. So "with the old corn of the land" (see Joshua 5:11) make a new way (creativity). Essentially use what you have to get what you want and believe the vision. Pure and simple.

The need to be able to answer operating questions about your business is more urgent than ever. Increasing pressure to earn more income for survival needs, such as education and health care, is real. We live in a time when, operationally, people realize that relying solely on their beliefs and abilities will supply only their base operating needs. This leads to many eliminating savings and investments from the operating plan to sustain the lifestyle they are used to.

This also brings us back to the different degrees of freedom (income, class, independence, and investment) previously mentioned. How much can you do with the income generated from your efforts? Will it sustain you? If yes, for how long? Answers to these questions reveal your degree of freedom. Want to move to the next degree of freedom? Elevate your standard of operating your business. How do you do that? Deepen your understanding of the best ways to allocate your portfolio of assets, the five capitals: cultural, intellectual, human, social, and spiritual.

One resource you can evaluate immediately is how you steward your time. Are you spending as much time creating wealth for yourself as you are for others (for example, through your job)? If belief drives action, what does this say about your operating belief system? If action reveals purpose, what are your financial actions revealing about you? Along The Narrow-Road, these simple questions reveal the complex decisions you are consciously and often unconsciously making while operating the business of you.

Why Five Capitals?

My journey revealed a distinct connection between one's faith and finance. We all anchor our belief to something when considering success along our journeys. For some, it's their physical abilities or human capital (I'm going to work to make this happen); for others, it is their intellect or intellectual capital (I know I will figure it out); for others, it is through leveraging relationships or social capital (I am going to call the right person to work this out in my favor). For others, it is relying on their cultural awareness or cultural capital (How did Grandmother handle this?).

In addition to those four capital systems, there is an additional one—belief in something outside of yourself. Along my journey, I've come across atheists, agnostics, and believers. My role along The NarrowRoad is that of facilitator, and I'm focused on guiding others in the principles and steps that lead to wealth their way. Part of how I do this is as a theologian. In this capacity, The NarrowRoad and I, as its creator, seek not to tell you what

The Five Steps of The NarrowRoad

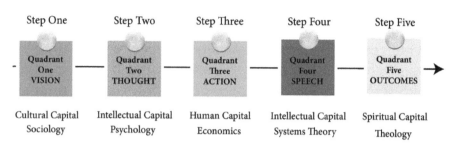

Step One	Step Two	Step Three	Step Four	Step Five
Quadrant One VISION	Quadrant Two THOUGHT	Quadrant Three ACTION	Quadrant Four SPEECH	Quadrant Five OUTCOMES
Cultural Capital Sociology	Intellectual Capital Psychology	Human Capital Economics	Intellectual Capital Systems Theory	Spiritual Capital Theology

to believe. The objective is to help you define what you believe about unseen opportunities that have yet to appear and their financing with all the capital within you.

The NarrowRoad is unique in that it seeks to reveal five critical components of your identity rather than the usual four found in personality and scientific typing tools such as Myers-Briggs and DNA, to name two. There is a capital associated with each aspect of your identity. Along The NarrowRoad, there are five steps, each associated with a specific capital. Each step represents a quadrant, with four primary steps/quadrants situated in a 2x2 matrix. The fifth capital, step or quadrant, is similar to the fifth dimension. It hovers over the primary four as that one additional step, that leap of faith that sits squarely in the middle of who you are.

Each variable in your identity carries a capital used as a currency to fund your pursuit further down the road toward and our relationship with it into categories of sociology (Q1), psychology (Q2), economics (Q3), and general systems theory (Q4). However, as I journeyed to make sense of the elements of capital related to the fundamentals of society, in ways that formed currencies we trade every day, some exchanges did not fit neatly into a four-quadrant box.

The Five Quadrants of The NarrowRoad

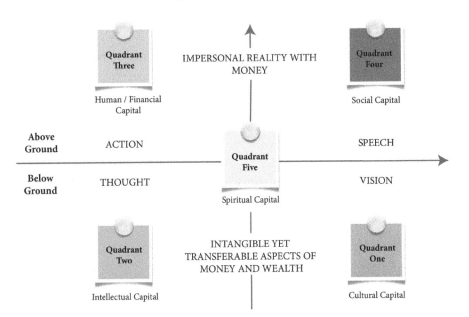

I thought The NarrowRoad method could be understood as cultural, intellectual, human, and social capital that evolved into systems and structures that corporately exchanged data, information, insight, and value. This would provide a means for developing a basis for anyone to chart a path from their current financial situation to where they decide to go. All it would take is a series of investments and savings strategies to make the required exchanges. Much of this proved true. But there was this additional element, a currency that was not as transparent but readily available and expended by all I interviewed. Something invisible, immaterial and very real. The NarrowRoad, as a result, extended its reach to include a fifth quadrant or element; spiritual capital or faith. Since what I found was that whenever most individuals grew uncertain about how to proceed or where to pursue something financially, they just closed their eyes and believed.

The NarrowRoad thus argues that there are above ground (doing and speaking) and below ground realities (seeing and thinking) to any and everyone's relationship with money and wealth. Above ground, there is a very impersonal reality about money, how you make it and how you spend it. Below ground, there is a more intangible yet transferable aspect of your view of money and wealth and your relationship with using money to build wealth.

The bridge between above and below is the fifth quadrant or element. It often connects the seen with the unseen and lends enlightenment, unity, order, and opportunity for independence in your relationship with money.

As a result, theology (Q5) became an integrative element in The NarrowRoad method. The preface of one of my favorite books, "*Heart to Head*," written by second-generation black theologian Dwight Hopkins, "sought to clarify the relation between faith and the struggle for social justice." In the book, Michael Dyson, a noted biblical scholar from Princeton, wrote the foreword and eloquently linked spirituality, religion, and theology in a frame I have come to live by. To borrow from his framework: "If spirituality is what they feel about transcendence, and religion is what we do about God, then theology is what we think about, what we feel and believe."

Keep This in Mind as We Explore the Five Types of Capital

#1—Cultural Capital

Cultural capital along The NarrowRoad is the source of your wisdom. Consider it equity that makes your perspective unique to your inherited legacy narrative and capable of shining light onto others with your distinct point of view. Many of us discount the value of our equity perspective, reducing the lived histories of our family to show and tell versus invest and expand. Within the American narrative, African-Americans share a unique history that changed drastically with Emancipation. What can you see because of it that others cannot? How does the wisdom learned from the migration strategy your family pursued influence your worldview? Remember seeing is believing for most. What viewpoint are you including or omitting in the road that lies in front of you?

When I first launched my company, I began a journey to try some audacious things. Many of the people with whom I shared my dreams thought it impossible. I didn't let it dissuade me. I shared my original vision for Torch with my grandmother Mildred Jolly, and she shared with me the disappointments her father and father's father experienced in their attempts at entrepreneurship. She also told me that because of these failed attempts, "I guess three times is the charm." She was confident success was in store for me. Our sharing shifted my perspective from crazy to soldiering on and executing the next degree of freedom for my family's entrepreneurial legacy. What hidden equity could lie in your portfolio of cultural capital? Have the conversation with those you need to. Perhaps this is what is required to fully execute the vision for the business of you.

#2—Intellectual Capital

Intellectual capital along The NarrowRoad begins with knowledge, but it does not end there. This asset in your portfolio may not matter much until you apply it. The value of your intellectual capital grows with applied knowledge, which means you have to use it. Education today is becoming increasingly expensive. It is reported that our nation owes over 1.5 trillion in student loan debt. The expectation that you apply what you learn to grow independent of the herd is becoming lost in the process. It's one thing to go to a good school; it's quite another to graduate and use the foundation and lessons learned to build success in your life equivalent to the success of the institution that taught you.

Even knowing I'm someone who learns best in a classroom, my father constantly reminded me of his belief about education. He was proud and even grateful for investing in a private Catholic K–12 education for my brother and me. He believed it to be the best thing he and my mother could have done for their family. But after postgraduate degree number two, he said, "Baby, the longer you are in school, the dumber you get." It was his way of saying, what good is it to have all this education if you cannot use it to serve and impact those who need it most? How and when will you find a way to simply say what you need to say to the people who want to hear it plainly from you? One of the last things he said to me was: "You have no idea the value that rests in your head. Share it with the world. Believe in your ability to apply it to situations and communities that matter to you!" In other words, apply your knowledge and be independent about it.

Intellectual capital is not exclusive to book learning or limited to a classroom. Your NRID will unlock your genius code to reveal how you best process and apply information. An example that will forever remind me of this happened while working in New Orleans with a client I had grown to love and respect tremendously. Every week I would write a report on the work I had completed and offer my suggestions for the road ahead. I would print the report and set it before him expecting us to review it in detail. What began as a frustrating experience grew into a treasured one. My client was an elder of the community with years of history in solving complex issues, yet he wouldn't look at the report. Instead, he'd look at me and say, "Tell me what you see." I would answer, and he would ask more questions. After a few months, I asked one of the board members why my reports were never read in our meetings. She looked at me and asked, "What makes you think he can read?"

Flabbergasted, I refused to believe this enigmatic leader, the manager of a multimillion-dollar business that spanned generations, was illiterate. I summoned the courage a few weeks later to ask him. He simply replied, "I know how to read what matters, Pamela—people. Besides, with all 'them' degrees, I thank God, I can pay you to read for me." Again, not all knowledge occurs in the classroom. Applying whatever knowledge you have obtained from experience benefits you and everyone in the midst of the growth and change that ensues.

#3—Human Capital

Human capital along The NarrowRoad is what you do with your strongest talents that distinguishes you from others in the marketplace. They say time is money. Time is everything, not just money. Along The NarrowRoad, your money is a simple equation: your time multiplied by the wage you can negotiate. Human capital is more than that because you are not paid for the twenty-four hours you get every day. Valuing your super-power talent beyond the value the market gives you is how you expand your time value of money. Imagine what might happen in communities if everyone used their best talent to solve pressing issues and learn how to build systems of exchange. With dynamic exchange and diversity of thought, everyone would feel valued. They may even learn to enhance their strengths with applied practice and new perspectives. If we learn how to better exchange value with others, business would not be a dirty word. Neither would corporations, which is just a group of people with shared interests working together toward a common goal of pursuing the primary purpose of business—wealth.

Despite constant compliments and encouragement for my public speaking ability, I did not like to play to my core strength for most of my professional life. I thought it was weak and not tangible enough. My professional focus was on numbers; hardcore analytics, which I was not very good with at first. I remained silent, trying hard to build expertise in an interest versus playing to my innate strengths. That changed when my most cherished mentor finally sat me down and said, "Pamela, you know all the things you are holding as most important in this job are things I can train and hire someone to do. The things in which you're most adept are things that come from within you. You know how to engage the client in ways that build trust and confidence. That is not a trainable skill. That's a God-given gift. Use it, please."

Biblical scriptures promise that your gifts will make room for you, and success materializes quicker when you play to your strengths. Those innate gifts are what maximize the value of your human capital. Your time on the road is a gift; use it in ways that create income and other opportunities. There is room for it in our community, trust me.

#4—Social Capital

Social capital along The NarrowRoad is about who you connect with on your journey and how you best navigate in vulnerable situations. In the instances where your needs cannot be met without assistance, who and what you know matters in the pursuit of the life you desire to live. Social Capital then comes into play when you realize that you will need to take extreme risks for your passion to be realized.

With ever-increasing social media platforms, the apparent benefit of your social capital is obvious, but the value, not so much. Look in your backyard and immediate circles. There is a good chance that someone there, or at most one to two degrees of separation away, can influence your pursuit. What economies of scale can you build with your current tribe? Before the ask, be sure to assess how *who* you know can elevate your standard of living. Often, you'll only get one chance.

Throughout history, the tribe, the group, fraternities or sororities are often the ones capable of building scale to match vision. Collaboration converts value into a chain that can support the needs of the masses, give birth to a vision whose time has come, and breathe life into a dream that needs support. Social capital is what takes you beyond the survival mode of life, but not without risks. There is work involved in building a great group capable of scaling your current existence. You have to trust and believe and wait and speak up. Your social capital along The NarrowRoad is centered on your fourth role in your NRID. Vulnerability around this role and responsibility brings authenticity to your social networks. It maximizes the value in the relationships near and dear to you. Hiding the need in this area reduces this capital into the shadows of your life. Social capital is reduced to who you know and how well you can play the game.

We are all in some networks where we can play. But for social capital to be of its best and highest use to you, you must expose more than the places and spaces you are great. What do you bring to the table? What do you need from the table?

As an entrepreneur for more than seventeen years, who loves to help people, this lesson in maximizing the value of social capital was hard for me. On the surface, social capital mistakenly is confused as a popularity contest. Once you venture deeper, it becomes an exercise of who can consistently be who they say they are. Leaving corporate America for a venture of my own was a daunting task, and staying within a network that was not pursuing the same dream became almost impossible for me. I remain grateful to my friends and family in my social networks who best taught me this lesson that I now share with you. It turned out that my innermost social networks connected to my dream were the ones who invested in me in the ways I needed most—even when I was unwilling to ask.

Social capital, when utilized for the asset it can be, is sacred. Along my NarrowRoad journey, I've had the privilege of working with formal social networks that have supported each other and their communities for the last century. Known as the "Divine Nine," these organizations set an example of what social capital can do when passed on for generations. While not a member of any sorority, I remain proud and inspired by their passing on traditions and legacy needed for past, present, and future journeys. Having worked with the oldest black fraternity, as an entrepreneur, and the entire Divine Nine as a banker, I have seen firsthand the beauty of building a net that works across the country and the community. It is a beautiful thing indeed. I reiterate, social capital, when pursued beyond the surface, is worth saving and investing in.

#5—Spiritual Capital

Spiritual capital along The NarrowRoad is found at the very places where there seems to be no road left to continue—a dead end. I've found that people use the term spiritual to distinguish it from organized religion. While biblical principles and narratives inform the journey throughout this book, they are meant as prompts for you to examine your belief system in the unique context of your story and faith tradition. Almost everyone, when faced with a financial challenge or uncertainty, closes their eyes and believe that it will eventually be ok. They are convinced it will work out somehow, in some way. What one believes is needed for a situation to work out is up to the believer. Any belief system that prays things will work out represents a faith in things unseen. The act of believing is when Spiritual Capital is leveraged. Some people have more capacity for believing than others. Most will have just enough. This faith is the currency that fills the voids between what you can do, think, see, or speak and what is beyond you.

Grow Your Spiritual Capital, Grow Your Assets

Along The NarrowRoad, genesis is where you start on your journey toward the inherited promise for your life. The journey begins with your family business model. Your genesis is experienced in childhood as an incubated asset of the family business, legally for up to eighteen years. This is the financial model you grew up with that taught you the context of a certain degree of freedom. An exodus is a choice you make to become the owner of your journey, your business model, which you will own for a lifetime (hopefully 80+ years). Your exodus is the steps you selected upon departure from the incubator of the family business to a business of your own. Each person may start at different genesis points and make different exodus choices that lead to different terrains in the wilderness. However, what is clear is that experience, training, and personal effort can take you the rest of the way to the promise you have both earned and inherited. Robert Sternberg, an American psychologist, said it this way: "A major factor in whether people achieve expertise is not some fixed prior ability but purposeful engagement." All you have to do is learn how to navigate the future with the capitals you have in your possession. Where you began does not have to be the end in your NarrowRoad.

Understanding the knowledge of growing belief abilities and purposeful engagement could address the income gap in our society. While this gap has never seemed more complicated, it has never been simpler. What is more important than the wealth gap is how you determine to best fill your gaps. Filling personal wealth gaps has a lot to do with our commitment to moving an idea from a dream to a mission that is executed to create wealth-producing outcomes.

Redefining Wealth with Legacy

Wealth is the value of everything a person or family owns, minus any debts. Income is what people earn from work and from dividends, interest, and rents or royalties paid on properties they own. In theory, those who own a great deal of wealth may or may not have high incomes earned from physical labor or work. Depending on the returns they receive from their wealth, those at the very top of the wealth distribution usually have the most income.

The top 1 percent of households in America in terms of financial wealth hold 35 percent of all privately held stocks, 64.4 percent of the financial securities, and 62.4 percent of all business equities. The top 10 percent of households own 81-94 of the stocks, bonds, trust funds, business equity, and almost 80 percent of non-home real estate. Since financial wealth is what counts as far as the control of income-producing assets, we can say that just 10 percent of the people own the United States of America.

Many people associate wealth with power, and while they are two very different things, they share some similarities. Power has to do with the capacity to realize wishes or reach goals, which amounts to the same thing, even in the face of opposition (Russell 1938; Wrong 1995)[1].

---

[1] Barbalet, J. M. (1985). Power and Resistance. *The British Journal of Sociology*, 36(4), 531–548. https://doi.org/10.2307/590330

Wealth can be seen as a very useful resource in exercising power. That's obvious when we think of donations to political parties, payments to lobbyists, and grants to experts employed to think up new policies beneficial to the wealthy. Wealth can also be useful in shaping the general social environment to the benefit of the wealthy, whether through hiring PR firms or donating money to universities, museums, music halls, or art galleries.

Certain kinds of wealth, such as stock ownership, can be used to control corporations, which has a major impact on how society functions. Just as wealth can lead to power, so too can power lead to wealth. The wealth distribution can be seen as the main value distribution within the general power indicator I call "who benefits." When I asked thousands of people to define seven keywords: wealth, power, community, legacy, success, faith and winning, I got thousands of definitions; the one most often was power. I asked eight billionaires how they defined power, and I got one definition. That definition was actually an applied equation.

Grow Appreciation of Your Assets; Grow Your Own Definition of Wealth

As a theologian, I have studied many faiths and traditions. I have found that during times of financial crisis and life's uncertainties, just about everyone chooses to believe in something beyond themselves. However you define God, the ongoing covenant and harvest that awaits in the Promised Land, faith is a part of the equation you need to embrace to gain freedom through ownership and inheritance. The transference of wealth across generations contains a tremendous amount of unseen activities.

Many business owners are slow to react to the need for change in an outdated operating system. So what does this mean? Do we need a new title, a new territory, a new degree, or more hard work? Not exactly. It means we need to work toward building our definition of wealth. One example would be to consider a new cross-functional operating model that values more than just your most recognized ability to do things—more than what is the job you are paid to do. It requires a view of your life that includes all the capitals within your portfolio of assets. It means believing that you are uniquely designed and resourced to pursue opportunities to expand, grow, and build a legacy in ways that include wealth creation. Your NRID is the key to aligning your assets with the strategies required to design a new cross-functional operating model to work smarter in the pursuit of your inherited portion of the promised land.

To build an operating model with wealth as the chosen destination, we must define wealth individually and work within those guidelines as we travel on a road that is shared by all. This way, your road will contain incremental improvements based on how you value your time and how you organize around that value. A valuation along The NarrowRoad is a review of all three of your financial statements (balance sheet, income statement, statement of cash flows), including all five of your capitals. Over time your valuation will increase or produce positive net worth— a position that begins every journey to real freedom.

Getting to enough is the first step toward creating a forward march toward your Promise. Having learned your lessons in the terrains, it is time to be about the business of you. It is, after all, an inherited business. Make it better with choices that reflect your financial valuation. How will you mine those lessons, experiences, observations, and messages?

Welcome to the business of you! You are the most valuable asset you'll ever possess. The promise is just a reflection of the whole you and the value of every last capital portfolio. As with every aspect of The NarrowRoad, there are dimensions. This step along your journey is no different. Action is the difference between pursuit and possession. Possession requires resources that are informed about who you are, where you are, and where you desire to go, belief in what you do and how you do it and grow the assets needed to create wealth. Believe in your actions.

Strategy Is Important

By now, you should have gotten my point that this wilderness experience is not a new thing in our communities. Finding a strategic way to break the pattern of wandering is. What is the best way to do this? Connect your pattern with the patterns that came before you. Put things into a perspective that enlightens your point of view beyond just talking about it to thinking it through. Use your capitals to fund your pursuits.

Lessons Learned on The NarrowRoad

Setting anchor points allow us to monitor the progress of our pursuits. Along The NarrowRoad, we anchor in two places: our genesis and our next level of Promise, which is your definition of freedom.

Learning how to navigate beyond the wilderness requires an understanding of timing and acumen around the levels of promise.

The three levels of Promise are simple:

Level one is the distance from survival to freedom. Survival means living from paycheck to paycheck and relying solely on yourself and the time you have been given. We all are given twenty-four hours in a day and seven days in a week. What we do with it determines how we survive. The outcome of a life of survival is leaving this world with good intentions but little fruit for those who journey after you. You did everything in the storm by yourself, and so it all dies with you. Freedom comes from choices made based on your ability to save and build and structure a life that includes a generation beyond you. The journey is shared, and so are the lessons learned and wealth created.

Level two is the distance from freedom to growth. Freedom, in this case, has different degrees, one being middle-class—desiring to work your way ahead through standard levels of earned income. The other is the middleman, desiring to own your way ahead through self-selected methods of asset accumulation. Class is a standard of living that is based on culture and geography. The ability to advance your position requires changing your strategy beyond business as usual, i.e., the circular pattern of working and spending. Growth is the outcome that comes from partnering with opportunities and dreams that share your pursuit of legacy wealth and owning a stake in the success of pursuits other than your own.

Level three is the distance from growth to expansion. Growth, in this case, is the now proven personal productive strategy that has and will work for you and now can be used to expand your legacy beyond where you can see. Expansion is when you have become the master of all the talents you have at your disposal. You can see how what you do is connected to what you achieve and confidently can model how to reap harvests that will last for generations to come. Your legacy is one of leaving a potential harvest in fields where you have planted a seed for future generations.

Here is how to survive in the wilderness:

- Step one: Write your simple vision.
- Step two: Run with it.

- Step three: Have patience. Be present in the meantime. Have faith it will work out as you work towards it.
- Step four: Recognize your life is the light in the future's dark places. Work your faith until it reveals itself to others and yourself.

Reviewing the Five Forms of Capital Along The NarrowRoad

The following will help you better understand The NarrowRoad you are traveling. Answer as honestly as you can. If you're honest with yourself, your road will narrow to a path conducive to your success. There are no right or wrong answers, even if they don't match everything you've read in this book. For legacy wealth to be attainable, it must be defined by you and the choices you understand.

1: List assets that fit in your cultural capital portfolio:

_____

_____

2: List assets that fit in your intellectual capital portfolio:

_____

_____

3: List assets that fit in your human capital portfolio:

_____

_____

4: List assets that fit in your spiritual capital portfolio:

_____

_____

Chapter Six

UNDERSTANDING CAPITAL RELATIONSHIP AND ITS INFLUENCE OVER DEGREES OF FREEDOM

So far, The NarrowRoad methodology has guided you to write your vision, make it plain and run with it. Wealth is a group process, so with your team, you will be able to:

- Anchor to specific outcomes and build wealth your way
- Build accountability to stay true to the desires of your heart
- Chart a path toward growing financial freedom using your unfair advantage
- Build wealth together
- Create a life that is abundant in the present and sow seeds for harvest in the future

Following these steps enables the development of an integrated wealth system to help you navigate out of the storm. Once in place and you have gained momentum, you are set to order your steps based on a level of financial independence you have defined and created a strategy to pursue toward a standard of living you desire. Before you consider these next steps, there are a few financial questions to answer and many to ask as you navigate your way through the storm you'll meet on the road. A storm along The NarrowRoad is when you choose to do everything related to building wealth your way all by yourself. Wealth is a group process. You must identify what is blocking you from getting what you need to allow others to share in your wealth journey towards specific outcomes in which you believe. Wandering in the financial wilderness remains a problem when financial illiteracy (not understanding the words of wealth) and financial oppression (not understanding your choices for wealth) remain roadblocks to creating a life you desire. Many of us are wandering in the wilderness between "I should know this but have no clue how to find out" and "it's much easier to fake it till I make it."

Wilderness questions that need to be answered. What should be going on in your financial pursuit of freedom?

- What type of portfolio manager are you with your talents?
- What is your work pattern?
- What is your lifestyle pattern?
- What is your growth pattern?
- What is your investment pattern?

The fourth role of The NarrowRoad is finding your voice. This step focuses on the importance of defining your message in building your definition of freedom in the Promised Land. Within freedom resides an understanding that you must maintain a standard of living that you desire and to remain there. To do that, you must build a better way to communicate what you want from your life. As my mother always says, "Ask not, and you shall have not."

Your unique voice expresses what you feel and want out of life. It is the energy that keeps the Promise alive and capable of transferring across generations. Yet many consciously or unconsciously remain silent, stuck between various stages of pursuits toward the Promised Land, waiting for the right time to speak their truth. Then comes a time when you accept that you are worth building with, investing in, and working with. You know you are there when you are unafraid to ask for what you want—to speak your truth.

Businesses operate within markets, and markets serve as systems for exchanges. Working within exchanges, one abides by rules and regulations, policies and procedures. My big idea required an established system that connected individual and community desires for freedom. This system would make exchanges between faith and finance and work to benefit the collective pursuit of the promise of wealth. These systems are nothing new. They have been present in the world since the beginning of time. What was needed all along was a way for more of us to take ownership of our role within these interconnected systems.

Varying degrees of systems such as these are why McDonald's is a multibillion-dollar enterprise with mediocre hamburgers and the local sandwich shop barely breaks even despite its amazing food. Both desire to serve hungry customers in markets where hungry customers exist, but McDonald's is working at a different degree of freedom than the local sandwich shop. By degree of freedom, I mean one's ability to do what they want when and how they desire to do it. In other words, the degree to which you can call and others will answer and ultimately follow. McDonald's has proven if nothing else, that it can consistently deliver on its promise wherever you are in this country or around the world. The new sandwich shop has relationships to cultivate, and those relationships will determine the degree of freedom they can and will have to operate over time.

While studying at Oxford University, one of my favorite professors, Dr. Peter Shelby, said, "Without regulation, there can be no relationship," meaning the strength of a relationship is based on the boundaries it sets. Boundaries create the freedom to manage expectations so that meaningful relationships can develop. "Without trust, there can be no exchange, and without exchanges, there can be no wealth."

Everyone needs a system of some sort to collaborate in the pursuit of freedom. To awaken to the economy of your life, you need to form a balancing act between your middle-class and middleman definitions. Understanding capital relationships and degrees of freedom they afford is how you structure your middle road to the Promised Land.

The following story illustrates a useful way to consider the capital relationships in your wealth creation strategy.

Imagine you are getting married, and the love of your life is walking down the aisle toward you. You stand waiting, looking down the road at who will be your life partner forever. As your partner walks down The NarrowRoad, there is a beautiful green pasture and a pool of still water. Just as your beloved gets past the green pasture, they glimpse their shadow in the water, and the distraction causes them to trip and fall into the pool.

What do you do? The choices are obvious, their meanings, not so much. The first choice is to jump in and save your partner. The result would be that both of you would be wet and ruined, and all of the people who came to see your cup runneth over with joy and thanksgiving would now have to wait for both of you to dry off and get cleaned up. Your partner would not feel lost or alone, but neither of you would be in a position to help each other by being stuck in the same pool. This is a perfect example of sympathetic capital. When faced with a choice to jump in and save someone, you run the risk of losing the very ground you have gained for yourself. Sympathetic capital shows up when that same friend who has trouble managing their money calls you for help with the late rent or some other base expense. As you write the check, you know this is not a loan but another donation to your friend's poor spending habits. It's not that you should not help. What would be better is, rather than forking over your money that took time and talent to earn, your friend would be better served if you extended another form of capital relationship.

Remember I said there were four capital relationship choices. The next option would be for you to get into the water at the shallow end of the pool and motion to your embarrassed and sputtering spouse-to-be to wade from the deep to get the help he or she needs out of the unfortunate situation. Your partner would not feel lost or alone but would need to do something to get the required help. You would still have to clean up but not completely. All would not be lost on your end, and some would be saved on your soon-to-be partners' end. This is a perfect example of empathetic capital. You know how it must feel to be stuck, so you're willing to lend a supporting hand to help your spouse-to-be get out of a bad situation. The risk is moderate and manageable for you. Empathetic capital shows up when you cosign for a loan or back someone up on a risk worth taking because you have been there and know the feeling. Helping in this way moderates risk, but if they default, it puts you in a similar situation as the one you are helping. While this can work, it's still risky business, and there are still two other options to consider.

The next option is to look at your partner in utter horror! Is this the person who is to be your partner for life? You may begin to question why you'd ever have selected someone so clumsy or narcissistic in the first place. You begin to unconsciously back up farther down the road, and you may actually turn around and head for the door, preferring to wait for someone who would not embarrass you. This is a perfect example of apathetic capital. Apathetic capital shows up when you lose a sense of empathy and prefer to focus on your needs or on similar situations and conditions of others in the same boat. A perfect example of apathetic capital is when you have done well for yourself and realize that none of the friends you grew up with are in your inner circle. You have lost touch or outgrown them and no longer have things in common. You no longer think the same way as they do, and therefore, there is no need to know each other's situations, dreams or aspirations. This type of approach, in some instances, is the best way individuals know how to get ahead. It fosters good financial relationships for the season, but if the winds change and the season shifts, you may no longer have that group of friends (who are only with you when times are good for them and you) in your tribe. But it's a choice along the string of options.

The last choice of capital relationship is that when you see the love of your life sputtering and flailing in the water, you run to the deep end of the pool. Instead of jumping in, wading in shallow water, or running the other way, you hold on to the long-term desired outcome and see the situation for what it is—a rock in the road. You hold out your hand and say, "I know this must be difficult for you. I know you are embarrassed, and yes, you do look a mess, but it changes nothing about how I see and feel about you. It wouldn't be in either of our best interests for me to jump in, but here's a way out of this situation. First, calm down, then grab my hand. Together we'll figure out a way to get out of this pool. I promise soon we'll be back on the road to the future envisioned and prayed so hard for. While you get cleaned up, I'll entertain our guests and plan a way to laugh about this later." This is a perfect example of compassionate capital, acknowledging the current situation and offering a strategy to get past the fear of resuming the vision as intended.

Sympathetic, Empathetic, Apathetic, and Compassionate capital relationships are at work in *all* of our communities. Those who refuse to engage in certain capital relationships can appear to be heartless or cruel. Yet it reveals what part of the financial wilderness you seek to depart from and navigate toward. Greater awareness of the impact each capital relationship has on your wealth pursuit can lead to increased levels of trust and authenticity.

Throughout my research, many people referred to the "crabs in a barrel syndrome" and remarked how active it is in communities. Once Facebook and Twitter are added to the equation, it increases peer pressure to conform for acceptance. After engaging with thousands of people about their desires for a better, more fruitful life, I have a different take on the crabs in the barrel. Instead of people not wanting others to get ahead and feel the need to pull them down, I believe a large part of it is due to people not wanting to be left behind and those who are afraid of expressing this need. Staying aligned, financially or otherwise, is essential, especially with people you care about.

Getting out of the storm is as easy as expressing your truth— what do you want or need to succeed? Some people may not jump into the water with you, but they will give you a hand they feel most comfortable extending to help you get further down your road. For this kind of relationship, you'll have to do your part. You must clarify where you desire to go, what you know is important to get there, what resources you have available to fund the journey and what resources you'll need to build to get beyond where you are currently. Not everyone will say yes to your request and welcome you with open arms, and that could be good. My grandmother Bessie Pearl had a saying for both acceptance and rejection, "Rejection is God's protection, and you are just as blessed with a yes as you are with a no, so pursue them with equal vigor."

Indeed, I have been so blessed by the rejections in my life. They have taught me everything from how to pick better friends to the importance of right timing. I encourage you to overcome your fear of rejection, which will be easier when armed with your NRID. At this point, I can help you better prepare for both your future yeses and noes, given that they are both blessings.

Sympathetic capital is at work when groups of people invest their talents into a crisis, often without a longer-term view of their anticipated return. While it may feel good to get the crisis handled, the truth about sympathetic capital is— plan, or you will fail. You will know you are in a sympathetic capital relationship when very little long-term progress happens, and the same problem regularly resurfaces almost at predictive intervals. People in these relationships are intense in their feelings but less effective in their actions to do anything about those feelings. I have found in sympathetic capital relationships that those with the resources and good intentions eventually lose sight of an outcome and lose control over their resources, namely time and money.

I was speaking at an event in Boston about capital relationships. In the audience was an attorney who, at one time, was wealthy. Part of his purpose, he felt, was to impact communities that suffered extreme poverty. When I met him, he'd been pursuing this purpose without a plan or a team to support his good intentions for about five years. He had left his lucrative practice to go out into the world to make a difference. The trouble was that his vision was not clear to anyone but him. In addition, this strategy was not developed beyond his belief that using what he knew how to do was enough to make this work.

Though heartfelt, his mission lacked a product and a business focus. Regardless of how accomplished he had been, no one valued him at the level he was accustomed to in the communities he desired to serve. He began to lower his standards and rules and regulations for engaging relationships. In his desire to be a part of the community he wanted to impact and fearing rejection from the very people he desired to serve, he remained silent in situations where he should have spoken his truth. As a result, within three years he had spent his savings, his standard of business sunk to survival mode, and he began to withdraw completely from his former associates and the community. When I met him, he was terrified of how he would afford to take care of the responsibilities to his family and ashamed for having failed so miserably.

Sympathetic capital relationships are akin to placing a Band-Aid on a gaping wound with the best intentions but not the best business and financial acumen. My advice to the attorney and to those who experience bouts of sympathetic capital tendencies is to:

1. Own your mission—where are your talents best contributed?

2. Commit to solving the business problem in ways that deliver a win-win; a win for you and a win for all others involved.

3. Recognize the storm and fix the problems you and you alone can fix. The storm is a short-term way to move people away from sympathy. Jumping in to save others

without knowing the investment you've made gains perspective while simply shifting your perspective to what is foreign and unknown territory. This leaves you prey to blind spots, which may threaten your current situation.

4. Poverty and solving the problem of group lack are big businesses. Undoing poverty and equipping individuals to build systems to address what's missing in their journeys to wealth is an even bigger business. So why would you not be business-minded in your pursuit of solving problems? Wealth is a group process that solves problems worth solving.

5. Share what you know with those who will not only listen but follow your lead. Gain knowledge by sitting on a community board. Create a how-to manual for those following a similar path as you and who come from the very neighborhoods you want to impact. There is enormous value in sharing who you are, how you got to where you are, and why you want others to follow your lead. When viewed through the lens of compassion, what can be funded with sympathetic capital can also become a path to a longer-lasting solution with a different capital relationship.

Empathetic capital is at work when groups of people successfully invest their talents into a shared need to succeed at something personal. You exert this level of connected capital because you have either been there, or are there, and don't want the personal reason you have come together to return. The truth about empathetic capital—timing is everything. Sporadic spurts of advancement followed by stagnant periods of low to no activity occur when there are high levels of empathetic capital. When the time is right, empathetic capital relationships are in abundance. Initiatives funded with empathetic capital never get finished. They address only the tip of the iceberg. They build momentum for a season, and then they dissolve into good intentions, never completely followed through.

I see a lot of empathetic capital relationships in the non-profit world. For a few years, the specific special interest of the time got top-listed for funding. Then, as quickly as it began, it ended. The window of opportunity for support closed. Those still focused on the waning interest field are left to fend for themselves. When the feeling is gone, so is the support and funding because the capacity to focus and interest to go deeper into a different capital relationship is not there. This type of relationship may not be all bad as it can be the spark that helps those committed to the cause get further down the road. Still, the ability to learn, save and invest in ways that will help in the future are key priorities to be mindful of while the focus and attention are on the topic of the day, but a pursuit you believe in. My advice is:

1. Focus on more than the ongoing support you are receiving now.

2. Learn the specifics of how the support you are receiving is being funded, structured, and maintained.

3. Build skills in the areas most needed for longer-term change.

4. Build into your message a call for a deeper level of relationship with those willing to be committed beyond the empathetic period.

5. Work with those lending an empathic hand to design milestones and outcomes beyond their participation in your progress.

While in New Orleans, I observed a lot of empathetic capital. I had deep compassion for communities desiring to rebuild, and I shared freely what I knew the next steps should be with those who took the time to ask me what should happen after my engagement ended. These people were ready to develop the skills necessary to advance to the next level of capital relationship. There is no passion in a transaction, and after the good-hearted people go away, you have to be about your business to succeed. After all, it is you who will feel the difference when the business around the good work is finished.

The Truth About Apathetic Capital—You Must Put On Your Mask First.

Apathetic capital is at work when individuals or groups successfully invest their talents into a dream they alone believe in. Apathetic capital is very much present when a few rising stars are surrounded by groups of people struggling to keep up within your community. At the onset, apathetic capital appears cruel and insensitive, but everyone in their own way must deploy a little apathetic capital. The word apathetic means showing no feeling, interest, enthusiasm, or concern. This is the position of someone solely focused on their dream and what they most believe in to get from where they are to where they have never been. To them, this means laser focusing on priorities for a period. I call this an exilic period where your primary objective is to build the confidence you need to succeed at what is most important to you. When we look at celebrities who make it big and seem to disappear for a minute, I believe they are building their independence to grow into what they desire to be in the community. For a season that requires them to fly solo, put their mask on first and take care of their needs first. Growth is change, and those in an apathetic capital relationship are changing their strategy to succeed in the future.

I used to ride my bike for exercise with Dana, a dear friend from Wharton. Notice I said the reason for our bike outings was exercise. Dana is an amazing athlete, and I am not. What began as a beautiful day of biking along the Schuylkill River quickly moved to me being miles behind her. In the beginning, I was hurt. I wanted to ride alongside my friend, but we were out there for a reason—exercise. My initial pace was not exercise for Dana, so she had to choose to be about her health business as the top priority. After I got past my hurt feelings, what it did for me, was to challenge me to build up my stamina, to remain within the vicinity of Dana's pace. My health rapidly improved, and so did our relationship. I recognized the importance of staying focused and staying connected. Think about friends who seem to disappear from time to time. What is it they are pursuing while absent? I promise you it is the growth they need to succeed at the next level further down the road. Your friend's season of apathy may lead to shared opportunities for both of you further down the road. Wealth is a group process, and sometimes someone has to take the lead to elevate the standard to a new degree of freedom.

The hidden beauty I've found in seasons of apathetic capital relationships is that you are setting the pace for others to follow, in their way, when you bike at your own pace. Don't stop. Keep it moving to the next level of capital relationship; compassionate capital. We'll all be glad you did.

The Truth About Compassionate Capital— A Long-term Relationship of Extreme Influence.

Compassionate capital is at work when groups of people successfully invest their talents into a shared vision. Successful on their own, they chose to form alliances to solve common problems worth investing time in while remaining independent in growing their areas of opportunity. These are people who see far enough down the road to know how they can support long-term progress. They do it with talents that work best for them. Jesus was the master of compassionate capital relationships. He challenged anyone who believed to pick up their bed and walk. To overcome their infirmity and blindness, they had to believe that all were chosen to work towards bringing heaven on earth.

It's no secret that I believe in studying and learning from the past. Time spent with our elders allows the past to speak life. I am blessed with mentors who show me what compassionate capital looks like and teach me how to create compassionate relationships. While at my 20th college reunion, I ran into one of my mentors, a committed alum of Hampton and Wharton. From the beginning of our relationship, this man extended his hand to guide me further down the road. When I saw him at the reunion, I was so happy we got a chance to chat. He'd recently retired and was now focusing his efforts on strategic investments that would impact future generations. As he always did, he spoke life into my journey and offered advice on things to consider along my road.

When I left the event, I was tired. It had been an awesome day seeing my old classmates and mentor. It was raining hard, and I wanted to get to my car as quickly as possible. To shorten my trek to the car, I could walk through a dark alley, but my mother raised me to never walk-through alleyways, insisting I always take the main road. Even at forty-two, I could not betray that order. I took the long route. As I crossed the street, I got a nasty cramp in my foot and had to grab onto the building in front of me. I noticed the building I was holding onto was a new one on campus. As I stood there,

I heard my inner voice say clear as day, "Look up." As I raised my eyes to take in the expanse of the magnificent building, I realized why following my mother's orders is always the way to go. This new building was named after the very mentor I'd just spoken with! Not once during our conversation did he mention that he had a building constructed on campus with his name on it, no less. All he said was that he was encouraging the students to research the school's legacy at the new research center—his research center! At the end of his professional career, this man is still building infrastructure to guide future generations to see what he'd lived to see. My earnest prayer at that moment was that we all deploy compassionate capital in our own way. For some, it will be funding a building. For others, it will be writing a book or speaking to youth who will remember your story and pass it on for generations. Regardless of the how, we can all lend a hand in ways our legacy will allow.

What is your capital relationship with your community? What about within your family, friends, or peer groups? What shared desired outcome could you all work towards? Where can compassionate capital be a reality for you? Take the time to evaluate which relationships could use a shift in perspective.

The following questions help you better understand The NarrowRoad you're traveling. Answer as honestly as you can. If you're honest with yourself, your road will narrow to a path conducive to your success. There are no right or wrong answers. Even if they don't match everything you've read in this book, for legacy wealth to be attainable, it must be defined by you and the choices you understand.

Lessons Learned on The NarrowRoad

Question 1: Describe a situation where you have had a sympathetic capital experience:

_____

_____

Question 2: Describe a situation where you have had an empathetic capital experience:

_____

_____

Question 3: Describe a situation where you have had an apathetic capital experience:

_____

_____

Question 4: Describe a situation where you have had a compassionate capital experience:

_____

_____

Question 5: What do your community capital relationships look like:

_____

_____

Question 6: Where could you be more compassionate in your financial relationships:

_____

_____

Chapter Seven

THE TERRAINS IN THE WILDERNESS

From previous chapters, we now know that the first rule of the road is: The way forward is really back through, and that wealth depends on legacy. If your legacy is dependent on the cross-generational narrative continuing, that begs the question, "Where do we go from here?" Everyone wants to know what is going to happen next. Understanding the cornerstones of your expedition will help you navigate a smoother journey to the Promised Land. Answering the question above can be found by connecting the dots between the past, the present, and the future generations. Within the connections is a storehouse of hidden treasure waiting to fuel your pursuit. For each generation, the legacy narrative will be elevated to a new standard; a new way of learning, leading and investing in the future generations' wealth ideas and dreams. But to get there, we have to know how to navigate the terrains of the wilderness.

Everyone has dreams. Your unique dreams are like seeds that grow into the fruits of your promise when planted in fertile ground. Along The NarrowRoad, there are four terrains to navigate in the wilderness: who you are; what you dream; the lessons you are willing to learn and apply; and the solidness of the foundation you are willing to build. The wilderness terrain is best described by the Biblical narratives The Promised Land and the Parable of the Sower. Along your NarrowRoad to the promised land, the time spent wandering will be determined by how well you understand the lessons in the Parable of the Sower. In the Parable of the Sower, a farmer sows seeds in four types of soil: rocky, thorny, little or no soil, and fertile ground. Naturally, there were four different outcomes for the seeds that fell in his field. Those outcomes are the four stages of development one must move through on their journey to promise: Rocky, Thorny, Landmines and Fertile. In the pursuit of the promise, you'll travel these four terrains. Seeds that fell on fertile land, the perfect soil, flourish easier than on the other terrains because the soil had the nutrients for growth.

Understanding who you are will build the confidence needed to overcome your fears of the roadblocks along your journey to legacy wealth. For the Israelites, this took 40+ years of wandering to get to the point of navigating past their fear of something promised that was great. Should you decide to take The NarrowRoad, it can be much shorter. The shorter path is called a quantum leap and where the best lesson of the Parable of the Sower is irrefutable.

You are, who you are. Your identity is unique to you, as is your dream. Sometimes the pursuits of your life purpose will feel like seeds in a field, hitting the rocky ground. At first, your big ideas appear to proceed as you imagined until everything abruptly stops and the opposite of what you expected happens. This is a polite way of saying failure, or extreme disappointment. Sometimes your pursuit will grow through challenges of thorny ground where everywhere you turn, there is one snag after another, delaying the pursuit of your dreams, forcing you to pay attention to and prioritize what is most important. Sometimes your pursuit will hit land mines. Like the birds of the air, outside influences grab your pursuit and turn it into something unintended and, in some instances, undesired and hurtful. Other times, your pursuit will hit the fertile ground where what you dream takes root and grows upward, reaping stages of harvest imagined in your wildest dreams.

Not all pursuits end up in this particular part of your field. Other areas of your vast field contain beneficial lessons designed to teach you. Those results are experiences necessary for surviving the wilderness. It's important to view the wilderness this way to avoid staying stuck as you approach the roadblocks on different and varied terrains. Being stuck limits your choices in the pursuit of the Promised Land and can leave you wandering the wilderness in patterned circles for a lifetime, leaving your intended legacy promise for the next generation to sort out the details.

Building a solid foundation based on your unique legacy perspective overcomes obstacles found on less than desirable terrains, such as the rocky road. Understanding how to overcome your insecurities about independence and growth will get you past the thorns. Having a strong sense of mission and purpose overcomes the landmines. Knowing how and when to multiply your talents reveal the harvests in your fertile ground. All of these strategies are pursuits along the wilderness journey of The NarrowRoad.

The NarrowRoad model helps you build a journey of strategic pursuits because these terrains happen to everyone. Like the four turns of the wheel in the wilderness, your unique identity effectively guides past them. A roadmap based on your choices about legacy, independence, talents, and life purpose narrows the road to become your life strategy. Owning this plan for your life is how you will get to the Promised Land, despite obstacles that occur in everyone's life journey to building legacy wealth.

Think of the four terrains as cornerstones and pathways that lead out of the wilderness onto a road leading to your promise of legacy wealth. Vision, Thought, Action, and Speech are the keys to the pathways as you implement and navigate your roadmap. These four cornerstones are connected to your central element; outcome.

On the road, the journey one finds themselves navigating is somewhere between two of the four cornerstones. These journeys, as categorized, are the four terrains in the wilderness—rocky ground, thorny ground, a ground filled with landmines and a fertile ground. Exploring these four terrains will help you determine the answer to the question: Where are you in the Wilderness? But first, you must understand the terrains and the lessons to be learned from each.

Terrain #1—Rocky Ground

Terrain 1 — Rocky Ground

Opportunity One: Learn how to expand your perspective beyond the wilderness.

The Rocky Ground Terrain is the place where disappointment can be a friend to the realization of your vision.

Reflect upon a time when you saw something and shared it right away — how did this help clarify your vision? Other people's perspectives are important for various reasons. While in rocky ground you realize both agreement and disagreement can sharpen your perspective.

The Financial Wilderness Framework

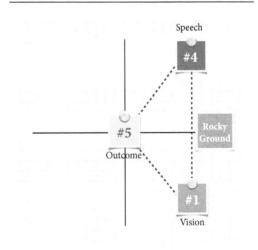

115

The rocky ground is the distance between the beginning and the end of The NarrowRoad Equation, located between vision and speech, or quadrants 1 and quadrants 4. This is the area where the tough lessons are learned that help you frame your perspective and give you insight into the areas where you are not yet ready to build the life you desire, as you see it. The rocky ground is where you overcome your blind spots—the place where you and only you see it clearly, but often others do not share your point of view.

The rocky ground is the terrain in the wilderness where you run up against the realities of wealth. The rocks to climb, jagged, smooth, flat, or mountainous, are the results of reactions and responses to your unique perspective concerning the order of things. The risk or the return on your idea will inform what is praiseworthy, what needs additional prayer, and what you still need to be enlightened about to build a life based on your vision.

The rocky ground in anyone's wilderness journey can be painful, yet purposeful, if you allow it to sharpen your gift of sight and clarify what you want. Some stay stuck in the rocky ground of the wilderness by shifting their attention from one idea to the next at the first appearance of rejection or lack of acceptance. These people become very defensive, unable to cooperate and build with others, yet they desire to do big things that impact the masses. If this is you, or someone you know, I suggest listening intently to both how they share their ideas and their reaction to the invitation to jointly pursue because there are patterns in both. Don't let critical, even when supportive, feedback that gets you nowhere, get you lost in translation. There is a message in this terrain for you. To find out the specifics of your rocky ground, visit mynarrowroad.com/rockyground.

Lessons Learned from the Rocky Ground Terrain #1

To leave the rocky ground areas of your path to promise, one must understand that every sharing is an exchange, for which there is a corresponding hire and a reward. Sharing an idea is essentially asking another to hire your eyes for the reward of seeing it through your perspective. Additionally, one must understand that there is a difference between prayer-worthy requests, and praise-worthy requests. Prayer-worthy requests are shared with those who already believe in your ability to lead your idea to fruition. They understand the order in which you accomplish things and are confident in your pursuit. Praise-worthy requests have matured from an idea into something more concrete. It can stand up to the scrutiny of those who do not see through your eyes, but can understand and believe in what is to become your ultimate vision.

If you find yourself wandering in the rocky ground wilderness, my advice is to take inventory of your rejections. Study your NRID system of success. Chart a path further down The NarrowRoad along the lane best suited for you.

I find that most entrepreneurs who struggle to make consistent income wander in the wilderness along the rocky ground. Their big ideas and desires, when shared with others unsuccessfully, are soon followed by repetitive disappointments. If a journeyer takes the time to write their vision and make it plain, when equipped with their NarrowRoad Identity, I'm able to shine a light on the details of the path that lies ahead for them.

Terrain #2—Thorny Ground

Terrain 2 — Thorny Ground

Opportunity Two: Learn how to advance your vision beyond the the delay.

The Thorny Ground Terrain is the place where confusion and questions that need answers are your friends to grow your confidence in pursuing your dream.

Your vision is unique to you. Navigating your perspective through thorny ground means learning how to unify what you see with the dreams of others. While in thorny ground you realize both how both questions and answers can strengthen your perspective and win the confidence of others.

The Financial Wilderness Framework

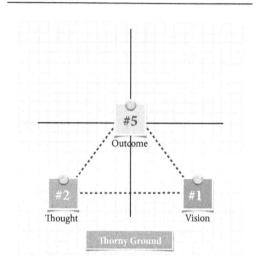

The thorny ground sits between your first and second quadrants. This terrain exposes the challenge areas that rest between how you see, and how you think. The distance between these two elements of your identity is a narrow one that initially triggers confusion and overwhelms. The benefit of thorny ground is that it organizes your way forward by forcing you to prioritize the areas of your journey where you must clarify and learn how to grow your idea into a dream. Dreams are things you can share. Dreams, once understood, build confidence in pursuing the road ahead for both you and others.

Despite the rejections and criticism, some of your ideas are meant to go further down the road. You know this is the case when you still are led to pursue it. You now have the courage to take an idea that you believe in to fruition. History has proven that dreamers are remembered and followed. At first, the journey is an independent one. You have to build the confidence required in you. To take your idea to the next level will require you to navigate terrain #2 in the wilderness, the valley of the thorns. Thorns are those pesky little details such as the wrong partner, how you manage time, or understanding if your idea is scalable. They will choke and snag your idea in places that are either not useful, or beyond the scope of your current understanding. An insecure mind cannot learn along The NarrowRoad. Your pursuit must have a level of understanding and knowledge to be successful. What survives the thorns, is what turns your idea into a dream.

Navigate Beyond the Thorns: Move Your Idea to a Dream

1. Write the vision and make it plain. Unify your perspective dream with proof others can appreciate, avoiding exaggeration and in-the-moment improvements. It must be written down.

2. Learn from what your challenges reveal to you. During the proving process, I found that everyone must learn and grow somewhere to pursue a dream.

   For me, my growth required additional degrees. I needed a classroom to build confidence in the pursuit of my dream for my community. For you, it may be other things. Learn what you must to continue the pursuit of your dream. Don't waste time faking it. Skip a step, and you potentially defer ownership of your dream to the next generation.

3. Obey the rules that govern the fruition of an idea into a dream. In my research, a pattern that became ever so

clear was that every successful dreamer I found had to obey three rules:

- A dream has to be tested by others
- A dream has to be understood by others
- A dream has to be able to be pursued with others

If your dream does not abide by these parameters, you're not obedient to the rules of a successful dreamer. True independence requires partnership with expertise at some level.

4. Understand the power of organization. Organization is the last thing it takes to move an idea to a dream along the Valley of Thorns. You have to prioritize and organize the elements of your dream so that others can share experience, understand, and visualize that which was uniquely given to you. Every dream has dimensions, things you can pursue right away, and others that will take more time, more people, more planning, and more learning to bear fruit. This was a valuable and painful lesson along my journey. While I like to learn in intense situations that resemble drinking water out of a fire hose, I found that not everybody agrees. I had to organize the dimensions of my dream for it to flow beyond the thorns into the minds, hearts, hands, and eyes of others.

The thorns are tough. They challenge you in areas you need it most but are often reluctant to admit. Malcolm X's journey along the valley of the thorns revealed that perhaps there was a way to share his dream with others he had not previously considered. His vision for the financial independence of his people was a relevant and necessary one. His method evolved with the challenges he faced along his journey. At the end of his life, he left a legacy that black student unions across the country picked up and, to this day, are working to carry it through. Not every journeyer has to go through each terrain in the wilderness. But one with a dream that gets through the thorns is almost always remembered. It is simply because those people have taken the time to learn key elements of their idea and prove its potential to bear fruit.

Terrain #3—Fertile Ground

Terrain 3 — Fertile Ground

Opportunity Three: Learn how to elevate your dream to a mission you believe in.

The Fertile Ground terrain is the place where opportunities unique to your abilities serve as your friend to narrow your focus to a mission made possible by the momentum within you.

Your dream is a recurring thought you believe in. Navigating your dream through fertile ground means learning to trust what you think and act on it. While in the fertile ground you have the opportunity to realize how your belief can drive the actions needed to accelerate your progress.

The Financial Wilderness Framework

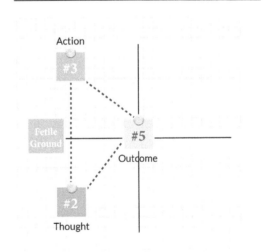

Hopefully, by now, you have given a lot of time and attention to the details that trip you up most along the journey. You are ready for the next terrain along The NarrowRoad, which is the fertile ground. The Fertile terrain is where you come above ground to multiply your talents by pursuing opportunities that are ripe for harvest.

The fertile ground sits between your second and third quadrants. This terrain exposes the fruitful harvests that exist between how you think and how you act. The distance between these two elements of your identity is what dreams and missions are made of. Good things happen in this phase of your journey. Doors open for you, and your unique talents are appreciated for all the hard thinking and searching you have done to get this far down the road. The benefit of fertile ground is that it builds confidence and faith in your choices and abilities to pursue your dream.

This terrain is when you take your dream and do something about it. Fertile ground is when you have something tangible to do about what you see and believe. Along The NarrowRoad, the lessons learned from navigating beyond the rocky ground, the thorny ground and avoiding the landmines clarify your idea into a dream and have deposited you on fertile ground, where you are organized and confident of the pursuit ahead of you.

Arriving on fertile ground means you are ready to come above ground with something the world can consume—your talents to bear fruit with your dream. You are creating a viable solution to a problem others can identify with and will pay for. This is called a harvest along The NarrowRoad. Harvests are returns on your seed investments of time, talent, and treasure (what you believe in most) in fertile ground.

Harvests come in three increments—30-fold, 60-fold and 100-fold.

A 30-fold return on your investment feeds you consistently when you put your best, strongest talent in the area most ready to engage it. Your first harvest level comes from the talent most affirmed by others (often in your third quadrant). It is the gift that makes room for you without any real effort.

A 60-fold return is when the exchange of your talents can benefit you and others. This 2nd level of harvest requires you to collaborate and, in some cases, partner with others who can see how your mission benefits their interests if they join you in the pursuit of your dream. This second-level return on investment is where you take responsibility for your ability to grow your talent with the expertise of others who may or may not know you, and they may or may not share your total vision. The compounding interest created in the joint venture brings this medium fruit to full harvest.

Lastly, a 100-fold return brings value to everyone in the wealth-building equation—those who came before you, those who will come after you, and anyone who is a part of your wealth group (the people involved in helping you bring the dream to full fruition). A 100-fold return is reaped when your faith in action has met a convicted belief that yes, you can do this, and you are willing to put into it everything you have (all five capitals). When you pursue your dream in a tangible way, in fertile ground, it becomes a mission. There are pathways to take a dream to a mission:

1. Go into Exile: This pathway feels like a period of exile. This independent phase of the journey supports what you need to get confident about what this dream is, what it can really do, and your role in bringing it to fruition. You must own the direction of the dream for it to be your mission. It was six years between Dr. King's success with the Birmingham Boycott and the March on Washington. This period in exile, was where he had to build confidence in his mission for his dream to come true. While lonely, this period in his life was the necessary preparation to speak life to a dream that influences the way we see things today.

2. Seek Affirmation: The second pathway is a welcome shift to a place of affirmation. Seek out confirmation of the strengths best used for your mission. Getting people to affirm your dream means that people appreciate the intention you are bringing forth with your dream and believe YOU can do it. You need affirming words from those who matter to your mission's importance, relevance in society, and reliability of deriving positive outcomes. Everyone does not have to agree with your mission, but some group has to believe you have what it takes to make the mission possible. Remember, wealth is a group process.

3. Take Responsibility: The third pathway step is responsibility. In this instance, responsibility is the willingness to deal with what the mission requires to move from theory to praxis. For a dream to become a mission, you have to take responsibility for it. You can't leave it up to chance and a few facts collected from secondary sources. You must think it through to the point of confidence. There is strength in knowing. A dream has to contain enough substance and evidence to feel confident that it can be realized, if not solely by you, at least to understand what and who is needed to bring the dream to fruition. That is where the partnership and growth into a mission-driven wealth builder begins.

4. Unblind Your Faith: The last pathway of turning a dream into a mission is faith. It is not blind faith, but faith unblinded by the rocks and the thorns that got you here. Your confidence level fuels your belief that when you do what you know how to do, using your talents and embracing unique opportunities, God will do what you cannot to see you through to the harvests further down your road. Often, they appear through partnerships and

collaborations with other like-minded believers in the mission and vision of your dream.

When Rev. Dr. Martin Luther King stepped up to the podium at the March on Washington, he was prepared. He had a speech that outlined what he wanted to convey. It was Mahalia Jackson who interrupted his perfectly crafted message with the urging, "Tell them about your dream! Martin, tell them about your dream!" The partnership with those who stood with him in his moment gave him the fire to fuel his faith that, yes, it was time to share his dream. Yes, he was ready, and yes, there were supporters who would take hold of the vision his life and legacy had made.

Terrain #4—Landmines

Terrain 4 — Landmines

Opportunity Four: Learn how to expand your perspective beyond the wilderness.

The Landmine Terrain is the place where triggers and chaos are your friends to help you navigate beyond your fear of success. Navigating the landmines requires the dicispline to say what you mean and mean what you say, it is where your actions often speak louder than words.

It's one thing to do what you want alone. It's quite another to want to do what you want with others to scale your purpose in life. Building the discipline to face your fears and your truth is the blessing of the landmines.

The Financial Wilderness Framework

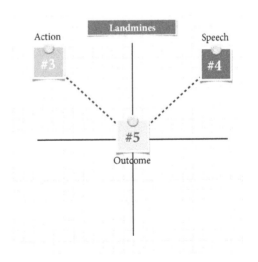

In the Parable of the Sower, the landmine is where the birds of the air pick up the seeds before they even have a chance to take root. Landmines sit between your third and fourth quadrants. This terrain exposes the trigger points that exist between how you act, and how you speak and engage others. The distance between these two elements of your identity is what defines the road ahead of you, the wealth within you, and the life you desire to live. In this phase of your journey, you are vulnerable when you least expect it. In the landmines, you are surrounded by people who love you, sharing the words that matter to your truth. This terrain gives rise to invitations for those around you to exert the courage to share what they really feel about the work you are doing, and want to do. The benefit of the land-mines is that it trips you in the exact areas you need to focus on and forces you to face the true desires of your heart so that you can deal with what it's going to take to attain them.

You will know you are in the landmines when you understand your mission, have affirmed your talents, have taken responsibility to grow, and have even taken leaps of faith to prove that the time is now for you to bear even more fruit. The world is asking you now: What is your purpose? Why you? What else do you need to succeed at building wealth your way?

If you don't know the answer to those questions, then you are in the landmines and will be picked apart by the birds in the air. Landmines are society's interests that will overtake your mission and change it to whatever they want. If you are unclear about your purpose and how your mission builds to scale, you'll get confused and become distorted from the chaotic act of trying to be all things to all people. Without a purpose, you can be convinced to try to do more than you are capable of doing, and fears of both success and failure can lead you to focus on the potential threats to your survival. Even worse, the landmines trip you up in your deepest fears causing you to speak about what you want as if you already have it. Your mission could become a hustle if you are unclear about your purpose. There are four strategies you must take in this terrain of the wilderness. Remember, the reality is to survive, and taking your mission beyond the landmines means arriving at the real purpose of your pursuit of promise—to build wealth your way. Here are the strategies to get beyond the landmines to the legacy wealth journey you were promised.

1. Choose to Rebel

Yes, the first thing is to rebel. Not fight. Rebel. Fight means to take part in a struggle, while rebel means to resist the control of others trying to place restrictions or alter the full expression of your vision. When facing landmines, my great-grandmother would always say, "Resist the devil, chile, and he will flee. Don't waste all that good energy fighting something you already won—own what you see." You must rebel against society's pressures to say you cannot do this because you are weak in this area — you are doing it your way. Rebel against others' beliefs that you're not good enough, the idea that you don't know enough, or haven't done enough! You know what you have been through. You know what you have been preparing for. Enough! Rebel!

This kind of rebelling is against something specific—the business-as-usual mandate that no longer works for you, and the fears of people you care about being projected on to you. Scaling your mission is your purpose and elevating your business standard is the way to do it. Overcoming fears and weaknesses are how you do it. In the landmines, words, accusations, and questions pick at your fears. At first, people are afraid of what your success might bring about for them and you. No one wants to be left behind. If you have done what you needed to do, resist the notion that others know more about the promise of *your* mission and the level of scaling you can accomplish pursuing it.

2. Advocate for Yourself

The next step is advocacy. What is it that you need? To be successful amongst the landmines, you must learn to advocate for yourself. Unlike challenges faced on the thorny patch of road, the distractions of the landmines are not working together for your highest good. You must know the specifics of your mission so that your purpose is sustainable. Details such as your budget, the weak points in your system, and what's required beyond your solo efforts to sustain your mission. Complete knowledge of these things is the way to navigate beyond the landmines to your realized purpose. Advocacy helps you find your voice. After all, it was a shout that brought down the walls of Jericho with a message that had survived generations, encouraging those willing to pursue the Promised Land. Your promise requires that you advocate for yourself as confidently as you can for others. Ask for what you need to succeed at building wealth your way by advocating for yourself. Speak your truth instead of pretending you have it all together because no one does.

3. Understand Your Position

An understanding is more than an idea. It is more than a dream. It's a faith-driven pursuit of a defined outcome with a purpose that has worked and has been successfully bearing fruit. This confidence comes from understanding that your strengths and talents address both the needs of others and yourself when used in specific ways. This level of substance and understanding is what you lean into to demonstrate why now is the time for your mission to move toward a specific collective outcome and play a specific persuasive role in a community that needs you. My grandfather would always say, "One percent doubt, and you are out, baby. Stand firm in what you understand." Understand your position and remain in it. Doing so will pull what you need to succeed to your current situation.

4. Let Your Life Speak Your Truth

The last thing to overcome in the landmines is to allow your life to speak your truth. Though you are not there yet, you have seen the promised land on this journey. You are on your way. Don't be afraid to admit it. Truth opens doors for people who want to join you. There are more followers than there are leaders in this world. You will be amazed at the number of people desiring to share your pursuit of purpose, to find meaning in their lives, by assisting you in your pursuit. So, no, you don't have all the funding; no, you cannot have it all figured out; no, you can't do it all; and no, you don't see from everybody's perspective, but you do desire for the right people to join your journey and share in the fruit of the purpose of your pursuit. It took me a long time to get comfortable enough to pass through this landmine, and once I did, the real journey began.

I learned along my Jolly-Journey that everyone looks for a weakness in strong people, but not everyone wants to hurt you with what they find. If you let them, many will help you get further down the road. It's part of *their* purpose to help *you* along the way towards their promise. PLEASE, don't block your blessings. Let your life speak its truth. You have come a mighty long way. Your lived experience is a message your community needs and most likely wants to embrace.

For your legacy wealth journey to be strategic, the pursuit of your promise includes experiences in all terrains. While some areas of your pursuit are collective, acquiring the confidence required to build wealth your way is initially your responsibility. This solo part of your journey beyond the wilderness is where the fun begins. From here, you can participate in the group process of the path to promise. Wealth is indeed a group process, a shared experience that includes both weaknesses and strengths.

The four terrains in the wilderness are the cornerstones of your journey. But first, consider the statements below. Which best describes you?

- I have an idea for wealth, but when I try to share it with others, they don't see it as I do.
- I have a vision for wealth, but I seem to run into multiple obstacles when pursuing it.
- I have the vision and knowledge of how to pursue wealth, and I am working on my mission and receiving success, but I know there is more for me to do.
- I have a vision and the knowledge of how best to pursue it. I have experienced success but get overwhelmed at the idea of building it to scale with others.

1. Explain your choice:

    _____

    _____

2. How does history enlighten your legacy perspective?

    _____

    _____

    _____

Chapter Eight

WEATHERING THE STORM: THE POWER OF COLLABORATION

Nothing happens until something moves.

— Albert Einstein

There's an African proverb: "If you want to go fast, go alone; if you want to go far, go together." For wealth to pass across generations, it must be a group process—it takes a collective group of people, strategies, financial instruments, and plans to build wealth your way. It also takes an understanding of history, its patterns, and the opportunity the patterns of history create. Collectivism repeatedly mentioned in this book is an imperative marker on The NarrowRoad.

Everyone begins The NarrowRoad in a storm. Doing things on your own lands you in the midst of the storm and is best pursued with others who fuel your exit out of the storm. Getting out of the storm starts with a shift in perspective. To help you shift your perspective, each NarrowRoad journey begins with the questions: What is wealth to you? How do you define it?

What do you need to learn to feel more confident to build your plan to pursue it?

A storm occurs along The NarrowRoad when a pursuer, trying to build, leans entirely on their capabilities and believes they can do it all alone. Though armed with good intentions, eventually, they'll find they have no clue how to scale what they'd envisioned on their own. This leads to being overwhelmed with the work of creating wealth when creating is just the first step along The NarrowRoad. When faced with the dilemma of being overwhelmed, many shift gear and go into wander mode—the avoidance trap of not doing the critical and necessary things for success that lead to building, growing, and expanding wealth. Soon they'll begin to question if all they imagined will get done in this lifetime. In reality, it would be much easier to face and make the necessary forward-thinking decisions of not going it alone.

At first, being in the storm gives a person a sense of power; feeling unstoppable, and since it is all up to you, you'll make it happen. While alone is great at first, it's not sustainable. You are limited by time and your own talents and abilities. In the storm, you believe the ability to keep inching forward is progress when in all honesty, nothing is going anywhere. Getting out of the storm is easier than you think once equipped with your Narrow-Road Identity.

The storm brings with it pain points that will burden you. When in the storm, what can be accomplished with the time and talents available to work with, is all up to you. It will become crystal clear that something has to move to get out of the storm. Often this is your willingness to become vulnerable to the reality that teamwork is what makes our dreams work — there is tremendous power in the collective. Because wealth is a group process, collaborations are apt to build a future more in line with the desires of your heart. Build a cross-generational team, and you're on the road to legacy wealth.

Getting out of the storm is easier than most think. As you recall, the storm is when you attempt to do everything yourself and avoid asking for help from others to build the life you desire. Getting out of the storm begins with a shift in wealth perspective and answers the key questions: how far down the legacy-wealth road are you looking, and in which direction? These questions lead to identifying the furthest future point you can afford to see. Is it now, next week, next month, next decade, or next generation? Is the depth of your perspective limited to qualitative ideas that sound good, or have you journeyed far enough beyond your imagination to clarify the quantitative realities of the legacy you desire to pursue?

Seeing, clearly is believing. Getting out of the storm requires a vision of the legacy you desire to create—not an idea of it, not even a dream, a mission, or a message, but a vision. Something concrete takes perspective and time to develop; time that began before you even existed. Once you have gained a wealth perspective, the second step to getting out of the storm is to develop a financial strategy. We all begin in the field of opportunity somewhere, and without an exit strategy, the field is just more wilderness. Without a strategy, it's hard to know how you will get out of the financial wilderness everyone finds themselves in at some point in their lifetime. For many, the financial wilderness is a place that one wanders for the length of their forty-plus-year career.

Finding your way out of the financial wilderness has less to do with options and more to do with understanding your choices. The NarrowRoad defines poverty as a life without options. While some chose to focus on the struggles of poverty in America, my research and lived experiences, have led me to conclude that yes, while some people are struggling with poverty, more are struggling with financial oppression. Financial oppression along The NarrowRoad is defined as not understanding your financial choices. A strategy is what helps you take full advantage of the window of opportunity you have in your lifetime. A strategy helps you navigate beyond the patterned circles of financial chaos and confusion so that the road beyond the financial wilderness is uniquely custom-made to your intended pursuit. You begin a strategy to get out of the storm with the second step along The NarrowRoad. History tells us there is nothing new under the sun; time and chance happen to us all.

I'm blessed to be able to speak across the country on the topic of legacy-wealth creation. Speaking ignites my internal fire to spread the message of our history, legacy, and pursuits. I encourage everyone I meet to consider joining the journey along The NarrowRoad to legacy wealth. One day, I was presenting to a group of extremely high-net-worth individuals and noted they shared the same hesitancy talking about money with friends and family as people without money. One woman said, "I can't talk about money with my kids. They might share it with their friends in school."

Wow! I thought. Imagine that. Fifth graders talking about money! What a novel idea. These kids might benefit from learning early how well a banker does at making a living and the successful methods Mommy and Daddy use to chart a path for their financial future. "Hmmm," I wondered out loud, "Imagine what could happen if the wealth conversation started by fifth grade. By tenth grade, the kids' financial perspectives of what things are worth would be different (Knowledge). A budget would be their friend by college (Action). And by graduation from college, an investment group would be the way to remain in touch (Collaboration). Imagine that!"

In my sessions across the country, I have found that when people open up about their relationship with money, things begin to shift. We are all navigating the same road to wealth according to our perspectives. Opening up is being vulnerable, and that vulnerability opens up opportunities for relationship-building not possible in the storm. When in the storm, *your* capacity is all you have to work with, while getting out of the storm is about building a team that sets standards to begin a more strategic relationship with money. This allows you to chart a path towards the wealth outcomes you desire and want to believe in.

Indeed, nothing happens until something moves. When we find ourselves in the turbulence of the storm, one thing that could move us is to find the courage to un-mute our voices about money, wealth, and everything in between. That we realize it's time to share our stories. It's scary at first to be vulnerable, but soon you'll find that vulnerability opens windows of opportunity you never knew existed. Ask any investor. It is the story, more than the financial projections, that can sway an investment.

It's great to look at long-term options: dream big, work hard and exchange with people who have shared interests. Together there is no doubt we will achieve more. Since each of us on The NarrowRoad has a unique NRID when building our team, we should be aware of the need for different, and complementary talent along the road according to the required steps of The Narrow-Road. Getting out of the storm means picking up the torch that has been left for you, adding your flame to it, and shining light in the dark places of value worth pursuing. It is also about taking the time to talk about what financially matters most to you, and igniting the flames of others to join your journey. Hence, the chain of legacy wealth remains unbroken and expands with those who, with your torch lit, can now see the road beyond what they know.

Now is the time to ask, are you alone in your financial journey? It's time to plan a way out of the storm. Survival is but a dimension of your life journey. Regardless of financial position, everyone begins in the storm along The NarrowRoad.

The first marker along The NarrowRoad is Vision. The second is Thought, the third is Action, and the fourth step is Speech. The last step is to anchor the journey to a series of desired outcomes through vision, thoughts, and actions. Without measured goals and objectives, it's easy to lose sight of the connections between past, present and future goals as you move toward the imminent financial and life's expected desire. Anchoring the bends in your road will allow you to continually shift your perspective from income to wealth creation.

As you'll soon learn, along The NarrowRoad, there are different degrees of autonomy we experience depending on: income, class, independence, and investment. All require different types of relationships with the capital you have at your disposal. As you grow, you become better equipped to manage the relationships needed to build, grow, and expand your legacy wealth perspective.

In hindsight, the storm is probably why some elders resist writing wills. Upon their death, they don't want their family to fight over their money and property, after all the wealth they've accumulated has resulted from their hard work, time, and commitment. The only one who really knows their legacy (and the wealth contained in it) is now deceased. Unfortunately, the result is their legacy creates the additional job of buying their parents' and grandparents' assets out of probate, diminishing what was left to build on for the next generation. Without anchors to remind us to shift perspective, we often avoid what appears to be uncharted territory, when instead it is one circle of legacy—the way forward is back through. When we choose to remain connected across generations, the wealth wheel begins to turn, accelerating its pace further down the road.

Looking Through a Mirror Darkly

It has been a constant occurrence on my journey that people, who on the surface seem to have it all together, will walk up to me and say, "I need to talk to you. I make too much money to have none." Or, "If my family and friends knew the financial reality I face, I would be in trouble." Grown men and women come to me saying, "If I go to my parents one more time for financial help, they will disown me."

I've interviewed countless people who have used their inheritance to pay off debt only to return to the exact financial crisis a year later. Imagine inheriting wealth that took a lifetime to build and using it to pay off short-term debt. A lifetime of building and saving, spent on a lifestyle of spending. It happens every day. This is how legacy wealth that takes three generations to build can be lost in one generation. The fear of facing reality about our finances keeps us in the storm, but on the other side of the storm is an elevated way of stewarding. A better way to manage what matters most is by having a more authentic relationship with money. What it takes to elevate money to wealth is a commitment to getting past survival mode and establishing a healthy relationship with money that can be passed on for generations.

Everyone begins their financial journey with a choice to go it alone, drop the torch, or disconnect from the journey and remain in the storm. Along The NarrowRoad to legacy wealth, you are not alone. Three generations of friends and family, bankers, and financial instruments keep your wealth-building strategy growing and expanding. The promise of legacy wealth is progress.

Each generation will do better than the generation before them. It's time to connect the dots that order your steps to build a system to elevate your standard of legacy to wealth creation.

Weathering the Storm Exercise

The following questions will help you better understand The NarrowRoad you are traveling. Answer as honestly as you can. If you're honest with yourself, your road will narrow to a path conducive to your success. There are no right or wrong answers, even if they don't match everything you've read in this book—remember, for legacy wealth to be attainable, it must be defined by you and the choices you understand. Understanding how to weather and get out of the storm requires understanding your financial journey thus far.

Describe life experiences, positive and negative, that have helped you prepare for this long-term financial journey (e.g., a healthy 401k or 403b, bankruptcy, a large savings account, a financially irresponsible partner, etc.):

What do you most need to understand about personal finance? Is it a model, a book, an advisor or a friend? What do you need to feel more confident in your pursuit?

_____

_____

What do you least understand about personal finance?

_____

_____

What was your relationship with money growing up?

_____

_____

Has that relationship changed?

_____

_____

What elements of your financial life do you need the most help with? (e.g., the doing, the thinking, the visioning, the connecting with others or all of the above)

_____

_____

Chapter Nine

UNDERSTANDING THE FINANCIAL WILDERNESS

Legacy wealth is a journey that connects the past, present, and future. On the way to reconnecting them, you will be assigned the role of designer and architect for the path you need to pursue to take possession of your promise. As a society, we tend to focus on the here and now. If this connection across time sounds out of this world to you, it is. Focusing on you in the here and now often leads to being unaware of the wealth systems functioning just beneath the here and now, which is but a snapshot of you.

What you'll discover on The NarrowRoad is that legacy wealth is already within you. Planted like a seed, it lays dormant until you need it. Though silent, it is a potent driver in times of uncertainty by assisting and pushing you along your wealth discovery journey when you find yourself ambiguous or confused. It supports its primary objective—to move you forward. To be a constant resource that fuels your fire as you navigate areas of your life that initially appear as uncharted territory yet are roads that have been chosen for you to access your inheritance.

Whether you are deemed successful or not, along these roads is the harvest of investments that legacy wealth made generations before you. It is equally important to remember that a promise of legacy wealth resides beyond you as it spans for generations, meaning you too are leaving experiences along the road that plant seeds for those coming behind you.

Within each of us is the desire to find the steps that lead to legacy wealth. The problem is that few find the steps, and even fewer take them. I can make this claim with certainty as I've heard this desire repeatedly while traveling the country interviewing men, women, business owners, and pastors about their financial futures, and their desires to go further than their parents, mentors, and leaders in their community. Charting a path toward a promise they would live to see was a strong desire and is why I was led to create The NarrowRoad. To help us tap into the desire within and honor those who came before us, I want us to get beyond the story of past pursuits of the promised land to the narrative of how we take possession of it! The Promise is then up to how we manage, operate and choose to lead the business of us.

The first assignment for the business of you is to get out of the financial wilderness and onto the path of a wealth system. A wealth system can be created in one generation and preserved in two. But it takes three generations to build legacy wealth, four to grow it, and five generations to expand it. No matter what level of wealth you accomplish, it can all be lost in one generation by simply discontinuing the legacy narrative that spans across generations.

Constants and Variables

In creating The NarrowRoad, as I looked to model its framework, I noted that key patterns emerged within narratives, legacies,

Variables & Constants

Your Wealth Equation

Along the NarrowRoad™ there is a base equation for wealth that is the same for everyone.

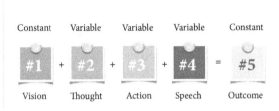

Constant	Variable	Variable	Variable	Constant
#1	+ #2	+ #3	+ #4	= #5
Vision	Thought	Action	Speech	Outcome

The base equation is biased by your NRID resulting in a custom road to wealth. The road to wealth is narrowed by both your choices and the unique way you function within your NarrowRoad™ Identity.

people, and groups that had found their respective promised lands. A common thread of each journey was that all included constants and variables. A constant is something that lasts, matures and evolves, such as a vision of your legacy or a specific desired outcome. Variables are situation-specific elements that can shift as you need them to, such as strategies, actions, and messages. The NarrowRoad framework, when viewed as an equation, takes into account these constants and variables.

Studying successful pursuits in both life and business, I found that the 80/20 rule applies to both. Eighty percent of all business is the same, and twenty percent is different. Really, it's true. In the case of life, the promise of wealth creation, the twenty percent difference is based on perspective, a vision of what is valuable, and what you think is worth investing a lifetime to pursue. In many ways, your perspective is your cultural equity—the value you place on what you've been able to see throughout your lifetime. The depth of your perception is the vision of what is possible and is determined by how far down the road of promise you can afford to look. For most people, seeing is believing. For a few, the ability to believe first, with the expectation that things will come into plain view, is a unique talent. Unearthing hidden stored abilities, to believe and see, is what I call cultural capital. Everyone has it, but not everyone uses it as a legacy wealth investment.

The gift of sight is one of the essential outcomes of Promise. Seeing brings about the ability to believe the desired thing is possible. Sight and vision along The NarrowRoad are two very different things. Sight is the ability to remain aware of your unique perspective and lead from it. Vision is a pool of cultural capital that affords you the distinct ability to see through to the next level of wealth creation—your next level of Promise. How you use it to deepen your perspective is the gift and the investment of it.

Along The NarrowRoad there are four types of visionaries. Each one with a unique perspective. The answer to the question of how far down the road you are looking is in the first role on your NRID. The first role of your NRID is how you initially see things. As a pure visionary, where vision is your strongest role. As a thinker-visionary, where *thinker* is your strongest role. As a doer-visionary, where *doer* is your strongest role. Or a speaker-visionary, where *speaker* is your strongest role. Your strongest role is what shapes your perspective.

Legacy is a Cross-Generational Narrative Through the Terrains in the Wilderness

Legacy implies inheritance. Inherited wealth is ownership of something passed from generations. In some way, everyone is left something to carry forward. For some, it is lived experience, and for others, its knowledge, social acceptance, financial resources, or an idea. Everyone is an inheritor of something. No one is left out of this passing of the torch from one generation to the next. One may not value or look for their inheritance, but everyone gets something. There are different ways to define and distribute inheritance. The pursuit of happiness, the American dream, and the Promised Land are all inherited narratives, that over time, come to fruition. The pursuit of happiness, the American dream, and the Promised Land are all different ways of saying the same thing: wealth is an outcome we all desire for ourselves and our families now, and in the future.

The notion that wealth could be created in one generation, preserved in two, arrive at legacy wealth in three, grow in the fourth generation, and expand in the fifth generation can be traced throughout history. Let's look at the #1 soup company in the country, Campbell Soup. They are a four-generation company. While many other soup companies compete for your purchase, Campbell Soup gets the benefit of the doubt every time as a trusted source of good food. This gives them the ability to grow their market share in terms of offerings and varieties. Another establishment to consider is the non-bank institution CIT financial. Within its 100+ year history, five plus generations deep, they have had the luxury of expanding their investment models into communities where many financial institutions refused to lend.

In exploring the powerful impact of legacy on wealth, the city of New Orleans is a perfect example, as it's the oldest inhabited place in the nation. Five plus generations have lived there. It is rich in cultural, intellectual, human, social, and spiritual capital, and demonstrates the power that can happen when families stay connected and pass on traditions over time. While poverty on the individual level was high in 2005 at the time of Hurricane Katrina, the New Orleans tourism business was roaring along at five billion dollars strong. Employing many impoverished people, it ramped up its culture as a tourist attraction. The service, hospitality, culture, music, and food industries collectively produced an income capable of sustaining the city. Known as "The

Big Easy" and a source of a good time, rich in cultural history, it exploited the moment when all eyes were on it.

Dr. King was born in 1929, the year of the last big financial crisis before the one we experienced in 2008. Born into a middle-class family, child of sharecropper parents, he was protected from the abject poverty and harsh realities many African-Americans faced in what would be the Jim Crow South. Within his small circle in Atlanta, he was protected from the lynching and restrictions of access to education. Educated in the North, he was able to see and experience things many other people of his skin color had not. He navigated the thorny ground of the wilderness for years, trying to unify his ideas of freedom with the dream of equality and justice. His books chronicled his wanderings in the wilderness, notably, *Where Do We Go from Here: Chaos or Community?* Published in 1967, a year before his untimely death, written on a retreat in Jamaica, *Where Do We Go from Here* was King's analysis of the state of American race relations and the movement after a decade of US civil rights struggles. He wrote, "*With Selma and the Voting Rights Act*, one phase of development in the civil rights revolution came to an end." The question of where we go from here is more than relevant.

"Why We Can't Wait," written in 1963, is a book that began with a letter he penned in a Birmingham Jail. It speaks to the power of nonviolent protest and why now was the time to pursue the promise of freedom. As a second-generation, Rev. Dr. Martin Luther King, Jr. sought to preserve the wealth, his own family passed on to him, in the legacy narrative of Promise that still educates, inspires, and teaches people on a global scale to this day.

Malcolm X's upbringing and experiences were a contrast to King's. Born in Omaha, Nebraska, his father was killed early on in his life. His mother was prone to depression, and as a result, he spent a great deal of his life in a system ranging from foster homes to various prison facilities. His primary education came largely from his experiences in prison and the streets. Intuitively brilliant, similar to King, he found his voice within the halls of the invisible institution—the black faith community. Malcolm X's legacy illustrates the elements and effects of the rocky ground, with his voice catching fire and sparking ideas in the minds of others who picked up where he left off to clarify the dream for independence. In many ways, as a first-generation, he sought to pass on a wealth legacy of owning your position in society and defining it for yourself.

Society's definition of wealth today is limited to material possessions or money. One of the main obstacles to building wealth is a lack of literacy of the real meanings of key financial terms. Its adapted definition excludes the core meaning derived from its original old English word, weal. An expanded understanding of the word wealth is "an individual, community, region or country that owns an abundance of possessions or resources that benefit the common good. This is known as wealthy." These wealth decisions build, grow, and expand over time with savings and investments.

Economists define wealth as "anything of value." The United Nations' definition of inclusive wealth is a monetary measure that includes the sum of natural, human and physical assets. Natural capital includes land, forests, fossil fuels, and minerals. Human capital is the population's education and skills. Physical (or manufactured) capital includes such things as machinery, buildings, and infrastructures.

To personally define wealth, one must know how to value their possessions. Possessions increase or decrease in value over time. The more aware you are, the more prepared you become to pursue the journey.

Decisions Are the Difference Between Creating Wealth and Becoming a Wealth Creator

Your financial decisions determine how far down the legacy wealth road you will travel. The first step of any journey is that of a creator of wealth. Your time spent working, benefits the long-term vision of someone paying you. In this light, you are a creator of wealth and a generator of income for yourself. The next steps along the road reveal the different degrees of freedom necessary to balance the equation to support your wealth desires.

Wealth development is built in stages and phases—the further down the road, the more opportunities are exposed. There are many options in life, but wealth creation choices are limited to a few specific tools to build, grow, and expand the value of your holdings. Curating your unique skills and talents, increasing your income over your forty-year career, when combined with a lifetime of savings, investments, and a commitment to ownership and wealth transfer is how you create, build, grow, and expand wealth your way. The NarrowRoad teaches the fundamental principles of business and finance so that you can elevate your life to whichever degree of freedom you choose.

Chapter Ten

LIFE, LIBERTY, AND THE PURSUIT …

Once we have picked up the legacy torch, our journey is to run with it. *Nike*, the goddess of victory and the name of one of the most successful shoe companies, had it right: *Just do it*. Understanding the journey and where you are along the journey helps build momentum. *Momentum* is what is needed to get further down the road as you navigate the terrains of the wilderness. *Collaborations* are best implemented when you already have momentum. Defining your pursuit, and being *confident* in your mission, is how you build momentum.

Often people would say, "Just do it, huh?" But, do it where? When? How? But do it we must, if we want to get to the other side where life, liberty and wealth await us. After all, this is our shared American inheritance, and it is up to you, and your choices, to take possession of it.

Pursuit is the action of following or pursuing someone or something. On The NarrowRoad, pursuit is navigating beyond the generations that came before us, and is the next link of the value chain that leads toward legacy wealth. Pursuit in action answers the question, where do we do from here?

This question is borrowed from one of the prophetic narratives that set the wisdom of The NarrowRoad, that of Dr. Martin Luther King Jr. He left us this legacy when he wisely did not leave the pursuit question open-ended. He narrowed it for us with two choices, chaos or community. Along The NarrowRoad your pursuit is designed by you, but the road narrows it to a series of choices:

- Lifestyle or Legacy — a matter of progress
- Chaos or Community — a matter of stewardship
- Fast or Far — a matter of trust
- Surface or Deep — a matter of leadership
- Baby Steps or Quantum Leap — a matter of accountability

Each choice reveals a part of the road that is often less traveled.

Choice One: Lifestyle or Legacy

There are two positions along the road to wealth. Midpoint and the Long Road. This 2-step journey along The NarrowRoad leads to the midpoint. Its outcome depends on the position you choose and determines how far down the road you desire to navigate. Choose a lifestyle of the midpoint, and the pursuit desired is to live a comfortable, sustainable life that financially dies with you. This choice leaves an impression on others and may even set standards others will want to live by, but the owner completely uses up the financial value of this choice. When you die, you leave those who remember great memories. Choose legacy, and the pursuit is the desired outcome to expand the family business model to the next degree of freedom. It requires navigating beyond comfortable towards a degree of freedom that includes the independence that only ownership can bring. This is a four-step journey along The NarrowRoad. Choosing legacy along the road means that financially you will leave this world better off than you found it by passing the torch of ownership to the next generation.

Choice Two: Chaos or Community

Along The NarrowRoad to wealth, there are two ways to go about pursuing change—Chaos or Community. Choosing chaos is often an unconscious, but well-intentioned pursuit, with very little stewardship of time and money. You find yourself saying (and believing), "I alone can fix it," and then you try to do just that. The chaos is that the "it that needs fixing" requires more than the 24-hours and seven days a week available to you. In the end, it drains all five of your capitals. Burnout is inevitable, and disappointment is a distant second cousin. In the moment, you are on fire trying to make it happen with not much accomplished. Choosing community is often something you have to convince yourself about repeatedly. This is a matter of stewarding your relationships in ways that produce what I call a win-win. It is hard to work collectively. Not everyone will see it your way. Nor will they think it your way. Even fewer will do it your way, but they will use the same words to describe it. Wealth is a group process. The choice of community builds economies of scope, scale, growth and momentum. It may not work right away the right way, but it works in a way that you alone cannot.

Choice Three: Fast or Far

Along The NarrowRoad there are two methods of navigating your journey to wealth as a legacy—Fast or Far. Choosing fast is deciding to go it alone, your way all the way, every day. It is the choice to trust the one that is always there—you. Choosing far is determining that friends and family are the first forms of investment, in what is, a cross-generational journey. It's choosing to trust the generational wealth process, despite what society may say or lead you to believe. Are there times when the fast method will get you to where you want to go? Of course! Use it when you need to trust yourself. Do me a favor here...sit and listen to your innermost heart's desire. Ask yourself if your ultimate desired outcome is to go as far down the road as you want, and if that answer is yes, don't go it alone. Take your friends, family and experts with you (trust the generational wealth process). All things take time.

Choice Four: Surface or Deep

Along The NarrowRoad, there are two depths of perspective, the surface and the deep. The surface is above ground; it contains things you can see, such as what people do (quadrant #3) and what people say (quadrant #4). Living confined within a surface-level perspective limits one's pursuit to time and relationships. While these are very important, they are only a piece of the wealth-building equation. The deep is "below ground"; it operates the things that require thought (Quadrant #2) and vision (Quadrant #1). Expanding your perspective to include the deep allows you to uncover the hidden treasure found in culture and intellect. Going beneath the surface adds weight to what people can see or hear. It gives the clarity and confidence, needed to go whatever distance you choose, to build wealth as a legacy.

Choice Five: Baby Steps or Quantum Leap

Along The NarrowRoad, it takes three generations to build legacy wealth and only one to lose it. You inherit a generational perspective of wealth and are also born into a collective generational perspective of wealth. This duality is often the cause of much of the wealth tension in families and communities. A choice to take a baby step is choosing to be accountable solely to your hopes and dreams, going with the generational flow of life. Choosing to take a quantum leap is expanding the accountability of your hopes and dreams to include the ways and means of others who have come before you and will come after you. The quantum leap is an elevated pace, as it requires the inclusion of account-ability to others for a legacy outcome that is inclusive of your dream, and those of others too.

My initial research journey spanned nine years. Imagine. Year after year, hearing the same responses concerning why wealth would remain an idea or a dream deferred to the next genera-tion. The patterns of my Jolly-Journey revealed four primary issues blocking our pursuits of wealth:

- Trust
- Access to capital
- Leadership
- Accountability

Here are the real roadblocks that lie beneath the surface of those primary issues:

- Lack of organization
- Lack of acumen
- Lack of leadership
- Lack of purpose

What is in the way of your pursuit? Is it an inability to trust others with your innermost hopes and dreams? Or is it a lack of capital to fund what you want in life and legacy? Perhaps it is a need for a model to show the way, or the need for guardrails to keep you on your NarrowRoad. What lies underneath that roadblock is the design for your pursuit (which is all a matter of your choices). Your NRID is the key that unlocks these obstacles in your life so that you can move forward and pursue the opportunities that live in your answer to Dr. King's question: Where do you go from here? What is it that you can't see clearly? A roadblock along the road to wealth is just a choice.

The road to wealth is narrow. Few find the path to fund it in time to enjoy it. Finding it early is ideal, but finding it is critical to navigating out of the financial wilderness. Right now, you might have a story that details your family journey to date, but do you have a narrative?

A narrative along The NarrowRoad is different from a story. We all have stories. Stories follow the loop of a beginning, a middle, and an end. But Legacy Narratives never end. They shine a light forward, extending an invitation to the inheritor of the legacy to carry the never-ending story forward. As such, it is important to know your story. Connect it to the stories that came before you with a narrative and uncover the forward movement leading to the necessary steps for the business of you. *Old folks say the way forward is back through (that's wisdom, by the way).*

Life, Liberty, and Wealth is in the Pursuit …

"That all men are by nature equally free and independent and have certain inherent rights, of which, when they enter into a state of society, they cannot, by any compact, deprive or divest their posterity; namely, the enjoyment of life and liberty, with the means of acquiring and possessing property, and pursuing and obtaining happiness and safety."

— *Virginia Declaration of Rights*

The idea of entrepreneurship, and its role in the next chapter of our American future, is an interesting one to consider. Entrepreneurship could perhaps be a road worth considering for those yet to enter the degree of freedom desired. This road, both challenging and rewarding, requires great planning action and determination. I have pursued ownership through entrepreneurship for the past seventeen years and have found that history is an entrepreneur's best teacher.

Within the Declaration of Independence rests a well-known phrase: "Life, liberty, and the pursuit of happiness." Some consider it one of the most well-crafted, influential sentences in the English language. The phrase is meant to epitomize the "*inalienable rights*" with which the *Creator* endowed all human beings and governments instituted for their protection.

Originally penned by George Mason, this phrase and its derivatives, known as the Mason Concept, became living law in every American Constitution and is now in every constitution except those of Russia, Mongolia, Ukraine, and Guatemala. As the Mason Concept traveled along the global lane, whispers substituted the doctrine of equality of birth for the common-sense doctrine of equality of freedom and independence. The whisperers also substituted a vague "pursuit of happiness" for the "ownership of property and attainment of happiness."

Here is the original as Mason wrote it: "That all men are born equally free and independent, and have certain inherent natural rights, of which they cannot, by any compact, deprive, or divest their posterity; among which are the enjoyment of life and liberty, with the means of acquiring and possessing property, and pursuing and obtaining happiness and safety."

Without attainment, the pursuit of happiness can be costly and painful. Happiness and safety may not be obtained in this world without "the means of acquiring and possessing property."

For some reason, this association was discarded for the more general phrasing "pursuit of happiness," leaving most businesses illiterate to the relationship between the pursuit of happiness and ownership. And the whisper continues. Ownership is becoming lost in the affordability shuffle, and with it, wealth becomes a tagline for those who own what most consider more useful to rent.

I live in an area that for decades was made up of beautiful, small homes and a few apartment buildings by the river. The community near the highway was quiet, tucked away, adjacent to the downtown city. During the pandemic, when it appeared no one was working and everyone was isolating at home for safety, two large skyscraper buildings popped up offering luxurious apartments for rent, and a new supermarket. As the rental opportunities increased in my neighborhood, so did the prices, and the home prices increased, creating more wealth for the owners. Is everyone in my community happy to live here? Perhaps, we are by the river, and it's beautiful. Is everyone building wealth with each new development in the neighborhood? No, this type of wealth is created by owners of the homes in the community. Are the renters paying more than the owners to live here? Probably, given the low-interest rates, it's often cheaper to own than to rent monthly. Are the owners bothered by the changes in their community with the influx of all these renters? Perhaps, they can always sell and take their wealth elsewhere if and when it becomes unbearable.

When I first published this book in 2014, we were about six years into the "gig economy," a term coined by New York editor Tina Brown in 2009. The gig economy began in response to the economic downturn of 2007-2008. I imagine the "happiness" factor of the gig economy is primarily due to the freedom to hold several freelance jobs, and live flexible lives, often outside of the office, on your terms. The gig economy disrupted our economy in that it changed the way earning a living was possible. "Hustle" essentially got a business upgrade. I re-entered the workforce post-Wharton at the end of the dot-com era. The gig economy, from my perspective, leveraged lessons from that era. It provides opportunities for people to leverage collaborative technology, to earn a living virtually. It also provides opportunities for group processes to disrupt areas of our economy that have not changed in generations, such as Uber and taxis, food shopping and delivery.

The ability to make the most out of your 24-hours, seven days a week to complete and negotiate make many people happy. The gig economy from a NarrowRoad perspective allows for the "surface level" of the road to wealth to be more accessible to more people. The ability to work when you want to work, and earn a living to suit your needs, can bring a tremendous amount of happiness. What lies hidden in the "deep" is what keeps many in the gig economy close to, but not yet, on their pursuit of wealth as a legacy. Necessary things such as promotions, healthcare, insurance, retirement savings, paid vacation, and sick leave are left out of a gig economy. These are the things that ownership of both the business of you, and a sustainable lifestyle require. During the pandemic, business owners without payroll, a banking relationship, and or employees were at first left out of consideration for necessary resources as the entire world shut down. The owners of businesses with systems for wealth were the focus of the much-needed federal aid of the PPP loan. It kept many business owners and their employees in business despite not working. I'm reminded of the lived reality of the formerly enslaved Africans post-emancipation, who were free in the body to do as they pleased; but soon found that the pursuit of freedom was not free. Sharecropping as a business model (the ability to work on land you did not own in the hopes of a harvest) became a part of the journey to build wealth your way. Sharecropping was hard work that often yielded break-even provisions, leaving the wealth journey unfinished. The bottom line is that happiness without ownership is usually a temporary thing. It can die with you, or when the gig is up.

Root Meanings

I would like to take you on a journey that explores the root meanings of life, liberty and its pursuits through a business interpretation. I know that understanding the underpinnings of what it means to be an American, in the pursuit of happiness, is important for those desiring financial independence. Looking through the lens of faith and finance, what I found most interesting, is the enormous levels of chaos and confusion people have around the value of being an American and the level of profitability one can attain by executing their inalienable rights.

To believe that creating legacy wealth will be the outcome of your pursuit in life is a choice. The ancient path of business as it remains today is 80 percent the same. The 20 percent difference is your unique perspective of managing and navigating the road as you see it. The 80/20 rule is always in play in business. Wealth is cultural, and it plays a large part in the success of your business. The fundamentals, what I call the playbook of business, is required to see beyond vision to process thoughts, actions, and the desires of others. Wealth is a group process.

The gate to entrepreneurship is a wide road filled with plenty of options and distractions. Those traveling The NarrowRoad toward successful entrepreneurship will find few opportunities to look left or right for obstacles threatening to overtake them. They must laser-focus their efforts on the changes that will come from declaring their independence to win the race in their lifetime to finish their pursuit.

I've found that successful pursuers/entrepreneurs, once they choose their lane, focus on the road straight ahead without expectation. They have confidence and are ready for the road that will lead to the upward climb of achievement and profitability. The narrower the road, the more you experience what you envision for yourself, others and those who came before you. My journey led to the understanding that the light of proven experience is never shed upon idea-generated whims unless one is repeating the same leap of blind faith over and over.

Ideas to true entrepreneurs are but stepping-stones to a better view of how dreams become materialized visions. All of which are views required to live a life focused on attaining liberty and happiness. Happiness can be found in ownership if you take the time to learn from history. America began as an idea of freedom for all that 400+ years later has evolved into degrees of experienced reality that is still not finished for many.

It may be argued that anyone working, living, exchanging with others, growing and expanding their family legacy footprint, and balancing all of that on a budget is an entrepreneur. If indeed anyone and everyone with a financial statement is a business, then the question becomes: Do they own it? Often the answer is no.

One of the reasons entrepreneurship is often avoided is that it's hard to find success and can be even harder to keep it. Owning the definition of entrepreneurship is essential to attaining its potential success. Unlike a business owner, an entrepreneur takes on an enormous risk to own a business. The path they first navigate is one of thorny ground. Filled with challenges, they have to prove that what appears to them as viable options can, in fact, be a dream others will want to follow. Success for the entrepreneur comes from pruning thorns that are not priorities for reaching the milestone at hand. At this stage of risk development, fully understanding the fundamentals of the 80/20 percent rule is essential. Eighty percent of all businesses are the same regardless of their functions. The twenty percent is the unique business proposition. Focus on the 20% rule, which is a patterned declaration when independence is the pursuit.

The Interconnected Strands of the Pursuit

A shared desired outcome of generational groups is legacy wealth. It's the continuation of the narrative of progress that did not begin, nor will end with us, as long as we keep the historical dialog alive, relevant, and flexible. Passing on the narrative is the inherent promise of a shared belief that things will get better generation after generation. Flames that ignite our lives happen very early in life, and when nurtured, they can become the torch we pass on for generations to build mansions or a means to burn down the house.

The subject of multigenerational wealth dialog is the foundation of legacy wealth. As I have intimately come to understand, wealth is a group process. Once self-defined, wealth becomes the journey of navigating a series of twists and turns, along a road that narrows with your collective financial decisions. Individual decisions over time that help build, grow, and work to expand savings and investments become your personal life business (yes, you are a business). When added to group efforts and multigenerational dialogue, it leads to a generational success story, or a lack of one.

Along my journey, I've found that everyone wants to live a good, fulfilling life and pass their accomplishments onto the next generation and to be remembered for what they'd worked so hard to achieve. Many want the next generation to learn the importance of hard work and its integral role in achieving a life filled with creature comforts. Many also want to make it better for the generation coming after them. I've also found that each preceding generation wants us to fulfill a promise that may not have been possible in the world they inherited. Sometimes it was hard to see how best to pass the torch. We need and want to believe the new generation will carry the torch forward to light the way that keeps legacy momentum going.

The saving and the investments aspects of every one of our journeys are governed by decisions that are not only financial. They also contain the tangible and intangible aspects of wealth. Tangibles are the better-known aspects of wealth: income, savings, owned assets, and a sustainable, positive cash flow lifestyle. Intangible aspects are knowledge, culture, relationships, and time spent remembering the purpose of our lives. Being a first along The NarrowRoad means setting the foundation for what will ultimately become a standard others can live by and follow. I have found that while we celebrate the firsts, regardless of the outliers who come along, legacy shows that every fourth generation picks up the torch and carries it further.

Throughout history, there have been well-known *chosen* leaders such as Dr. King and lesser-known ones, such as Bessie Pearl Watkins Horne (my grandmother), perhaps even you and me, who seemingly emerge with the inherited purpose to build and organize a way forward for the masses. These avenger types help make sense of the world we live in so that others can navigate with confidence and clarity toward purpose and fulfillment. Each often leaves behind the instructions of their times so that future generations have a guiding light on the road forward.

I'm one of those people born to think, observe, share, and record the progress of our lifetime. An outlier, I believe I have been chosen, or chose the task of bearing and passing the Torch, in my case with *The NarrowRoad* tools I've developed to help myself and others navigate a way forward. Make no mistake, you and I are here together, in this time, and it is important to the Promise that we anchor our lives to a common yet individual outcome needed to push the generational wheel of life forward. It has fallen to our shared generational moment in time to regain some of the momenta and mend the disconnect that has been lost in our pursuit of freedom and happiness. Yet more of us seem to be losing sight of a way to arrive at the happiness we want from the life we've inherited. It's time to reconnect the dots and navigate back to the promise of legacy wealth, however we define it.

How do you define legacy wealth? Along The NarrowRoad, this will be *your* ultimate desired outcome as anchored to your life's strategy. In the Bible, the outcome for the seekers is called the Promised Land. In America, it is called the American Dream, also known as the pursuit of happiness. *The desired outcome remains constant until it has been attained.* While along The NarrowRoad, *your* desired outcome becomes the guiding light to the end of your road. Every day you choose to move closer to your life purpose, *your* desired outcome helps measure the progress of the legacy and the wealth you're building, growing and expanding. Achieving the desired outcome means taking possession of an inherited promise by harvesting the seeds that took lifetimes to plant, especially for you. And harvesting will require an understanding of Capital relationships.

Chapter Eleven

THE LEGACY THREAD

To move beyond survival, one must earn more than one spends, which requires societies to consistently increase consumption from those who are free to create more income-earning opportunities. To move beyond freedom, one must learn how to save and invest in opportunities created by those planning long term for their (not-so-plainly-seen) future. To leave wealth that passes on for generations, one must be able to see opportunities in all the dimensions of wealth evolving along the road to wealth; following in the footsteps of those who came before us and are coming after us.

Understanding what I will call the legacy thread is what I've found to best assist people focused on financial independence via ownership. This legacy thread connects the core elements of America's business model. This thread is like a three-stranded cord that, if well intertwined, cannot be broken and has a history of leading groups of Americans to wealth-bearing success. For some groups, the strands of life, liberty and the pursuit of...have been tightly wound together for generations. This has enabled each generation to pursue greater degrees of freedom—financial and otherwise. For other groups, the strands, not yet attached, lie separated like dry bones in a dark valley. This reduces their pursuits to short-lived phases of promises that fizzle shortly after the spark of an idea, or seasons of consistent income. The following illustration desires to provide a glimpse into what is needed to link the three strands together so that you can find the value promised in the history of the pursuits of declared financial independence.

Your Life is A Business

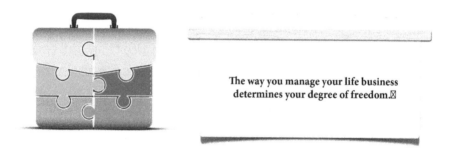

The way you manage your life business determines your degree of freedom.

Strand One: Life

Life is a gift. But what type of gift? For me, it's a gift, that if paid attention to, keeps on giving. In essence, it multiplies or appreciates over time. Looking up the word life in the dictionary will give varied answers, such as the capacity for growth, reproduction, functional activity, and continual change until you die. Put another way; it's your eighty-plus-year potential to create, leave an impact, or contribute to the current situation.

Seen through the lens of business, life to me is an asset—not just for you but for the benefit of others. Yet lives often go underutilized, undeveloped, underestimated and over-leveraged. Some lives are limited to current transactions. In this case, life is only valued through the lens of money, which seems more like a path of a hustler than a path leading toward legacy wealth.

Essentially, life is a value-based asset where its shareholders, that's you and your family, determine the value. If not taken care of, despite the body's potential to self-heal and one's intellectual and emotional capacity to reach great heights, life can depreciate rapidly by incurring liabilities such as disease, the cost of health care, and other fear-based decisions that further deplete life assets. Capricious living makes choices like fast food look like a debit to your balance sheet.

Liberty is Ownership

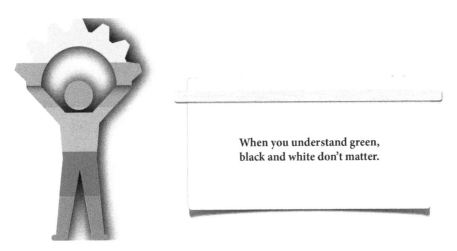

When you understand green,
black and white don't matter.

Strand Two: Liberty

Liberty is something some people take very seriously. Recall the phrase: "Give me liberty or give me death!" It is a quotation attributed to Patrick Henry from a speech he made to the Virginia Convention on March 23, 1775, at St. John's Church in Richmond, Virginia. The speech was credited with having swung the balance in convincing the Virginia House of Burgesses to pass a resolution delivering the Virginia troops to the Revolutionary War. Among the delegates to the convention were future US presidents Thomas Jefferson and George Washington. Reportedly, those in attendance, upon hearing the speech, shouted, "Give me liberty or give me death!" Indeed, many a war has been fought for liberty.

For those less dramatically inclined, liberty can mean the power or scope to act as one pleases. In other words, your ability to see what you want and choose to make it happen, whichever way you deem appropriate or can afford with your life assets. For me, liberty is one's ability to see and invest in the change they want to happen now. The right to rebel against, or support, the status quo is a right you own. The fight for liberty is a longstanding pattern in the history of the American people. Looking at it through a business lens, liberty is the equity you own and are willing to invest for the right changes or causes you believe advantageous.

Exploring the first two strands has uncovered assets, liabilities and owner's equity. When history is looked upon in this way, one's balance sheet can be found in the field where life and liberty are appropriately valued and invested.

Ownership is The Promise

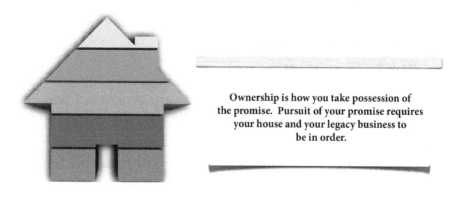

Ownership is how you take possession of the promise. Pursuit of your promise requires your house and your legacy business to be in order.

Strand Three: Pursuit of …

I have left the place after "of" blank because happiness is subjective; meaning uniquely defined by you. Pursuit, by definition, means to strive toward, to quest after, or to search for. It can also mean an aim, goal, objective, or dream. To pursue something is to continually strive to find ways to maximize your capacity to attain it. Pursuing can also mean building upon a glimpse of what's possible and remaining consistent to see it through until fruition. In this case, pursuit is similar to an operating system of actions and strategies anchored to a specific goal and objective. For me, one's pursuit is how a person actualizes their dream or monetizes their business with assets they have at their disposal. The object of the pursuit through ownership derives profit. Achieving a profit milestone means overcoming hurdles that move you beyond the limitation of starting from scratch, generation after generation. Your pursuit can be an income statement from sowing the seed of your vision (top-line revenue) and reaping its harvest (bottom-line profit/success) of your business. The pursuit is taking ownership of whatever you deem is the way to master a successful route to wealth.

Linking the Strands

The glue that binds these strands together is happiness, or as the author of the premise of American freedom, George Mason, stated: ownership. Happiness in America is largely based on the ownership of something. In the beginning days of America, you couldn't vote if you didn't own property. The way it is today, is that the largest owners of assets have greater influence over society than those wandering in the wilderness of financial management; often because they can afford to leverage their ownership to their advantage.

Happiness is subjective when left to the eyes of the beholder. It is often reduced to a mental or emotional state of *well-being* and often characterized by positive or *pleasant* emotions, ranging from *contentment* to intense joy. In our current business framework, happiness could be related to a business's condition by optimizing the use of your assets and investments. What underlies the definition of freedom and happiness in America is a confusion of what financial happiness means. For the American business model, happiness is increased levels of ownership in the business of success. Freedom is one's ability to afford the pursuit as one desires. The degrees of freedom you choose, build the levels of wealth commensurate with the types of risk you are willing to take to build, grow, and expand wealth in your lifetime. The cost of ownership in the American business model is taxes, property, income, sales, and estate. The benefit is that when executed correctly, the owner creates what otherwise would remain unseen.

Your derived equity through the operations of your system of pursuit, done well, could equate to happiness and joy through the process. Here is where this strand of declared independence (pursuit of...) gets interesting.

In a world where there is the seen (that which is "already done") and the unseen (that which is not yet manifested), both life and business include lives, liberties, and pursuits. At this inflection point, the entrepreneur must answer the question: Where do we go from here? It is the successful owner/entrepreneur who sets the destination of the pursuit.

So, one might argue that the level of happiness or freedom depends on the level of ownership. From a distance, the current discourse in America stems from ownership levels of the 99 percent and 1 percent. Up close, through a distorted business lens, it can be confusing how wealth is created and who should bear the burden of the cost of freedom in America. This largely boils down to ownership, which is a form of entrepreneurship. Only you know what financial happiness means to you. Prayerfully you have budgeted for it. If not, I encourage you to chart a path along The NarrowRoad. A budget is not a set of limits. It is a plan for executing choices and decisions you have agreed to commit your five types of capital resources.

Legacy Is More Than An Idea—It's A Lifelong Pursuit

An entrepreneur is more than someone with an idea and a slick marketing way to spin it. They take on greater than normal financial risks to organize and operate a business that can change things and constantly evolve. A true entrepreneur is someone who has the wisdom, knowledge, and understanding to braid the threads of the cord that binds the American Dream together. An entrepreneur along The NarrowRoad is any individual who owns a way to create a future we all can participate in, whether as a consumer, investor, employee, co-founder, successor, or inheritor.

For me, becoming an entrepreneur is a calling. Have you been called? What is it asking of you? Eighty percent of the call is asking you to take the time to value your assets, own your equity, rev up your operations, and define happiness in whatever way you desire. It is also asking you to remember to pay your taxes so that America will continue its journey to mirror the happiness we all in some way desire to pursue. I'm thankful for what my journey has revealed about the business model of America and its need for more of us to actively participate.

Regardless of the risk of your call, and the resulting influence it has on your pursuit, continue the journey to wealth your way. Remember, wide is the gate of opportunity; narrow is the road to success. If you are one of the increasing few, who finds the narrow gate and choose to pursue ownership with every ounce of equity you have, the best is surely yet to come.

The Legacy Must Continue

After years of wandering in the financial wilderness looking for clues, my Jolly-Journey again shifted its perspective further down the road. The death of my father confirmed this shift. One of the last things he said to me was, "The legacy must continue." As I observe the current and recent graduates of Hampton and Wharton, the parenting styles and the professional pathways of my peers, parents, and grandparents, I know we have what it takes to elevate the standard of our legacy to wealth. We just need a collective call and a road to pursue it.

That is what you will find journeying along The NarrowRoad—an integrated, structured journey that infuses our history, legacy, business, systems, pursuits, and roadmaps to travel further down the road, from income to savings, to investments to wealth, in ways that honor our legacy promise. The purpose of The NarrowRoad is to chart your path toward a life purpose, inclusive of its financial aspects. We are all, in some way, builders of the future. Our present is the beginning of future generations' view of what is possible. Fifty years prior, my American ancestors sang the promise that we shall one day overcome. In the case of The NarrowRoad, for them, it is the overcoming of financial oppression. For you, it is choosing to own your choices about wealth.

Chapter Twelve

WEALTH CREATION

Wealth is a group process of individuals journeying in a collective pursuit of desired outcomes that are similar but not the same.

Wealth is often explained in parables and stories with hidden multidimensional meanings translated by a cultural worldview.

Wealth is a series of exchanges and collaborations based on an individual's valuations.

Wealth requires a group agreement that builds trust and structure over time.

Today, society's definition of wealth is limited to material possessions or money. One of the main obstacles to building wealth is a lack of literacy of the real meanings of key financial terms. Society's adapted definition excludes the core meaning derived from its original old English word, weal. An expanded understanding of the word wealth is "an individual, community, region or country that owns an abundance of possessions or resources that benefit the common good. This is known as wealthy." These wealth decisions build, grow, and expand over time with savings and investments.

Economists define wealth as "anything of value." The United Nations' definition of inclusive wealth is a monetary measure that includes the sum of natural, human and physical assets. Natural capital includes land, forests, fossil fuels, and minerals. Human capital is the population's education and skills. Physical (or "manufactured") capital includes such things as machinery, buildings, and infrastructures.

To personally define wealth, one must know how to value their possessions. And possessions increase or decrease in value over time. The more aware you are, the more prepared you become to pursue the journey.

Along The NarrowRoad, wealth creation is a series of financial decisions that build, grow, and expand over time with savings, ownership, and investments. Your wealth journey contains options, decisions, and choices you must make to get where you desire to go. Our initial family business experience, the 18 years where we are hopefully incubated in love, safety, and provisions (our Genesis), led us to a point where we must take an exodus from the family financial statement, to somewhere on the terrain in the financial wilderness.

Building wealth requires that you first commit to the decision that wealth is for you. What's next is to make your vision of it plain, with a strategy that creates your unfair advantage. With a strategy in place that you understand and are confident about, you are now ready for the third step—assessing your current position in the financial wilderness. Once you've chosen to get out of the financial wilderness, committed to exiting it, and defined the level of wealth you desire to pursue, the third step is to uncover the resources you have to execute your most desired pursuit. You've now arrived at the point where you've fully come to understand and appreciate the business of you.

On the road, you'll learn what it takes to create wealth. In this case, wealth is a series of financial decisions that build, grow, and expand over time with savings and investments. Wealth comes with ownership of your vision, thoughts, actions, and voice—the higher your level of acumen, the greater your opportunity for wealth.

Along the road, you'll also meet Faith. Faith is a necessary currency and the glue of pursuit. Our elders are right when they say, "What is for you, is for you." I translate that to mean that once you've staked your claim, the wide gate of life, narrows and there on the narrowed road of choice, is your purpose-driven life. Few take the time to find their purpose, and even fewer take the road that leads to it. I believe the few who take The NarrowRoad learn the importance of remaining connected to the legacy narrative by picking up the torch, and taking it further down the road with unblinded faith. Living life in this manner opens our eyes and the doors of opportunity not readily available to everyone. It's open to those who know the pathway to their treasures hidden in the dark, fertile areas of their legacy.

Regardless of our individual desires, linking past narratives to our present life narratives shed light on our uncharted paths. To see the continuum and come to appreciate that our hopes, successes, and failures illuminate pathways for future travelers who will build and grow their inheritance, is legacy's purpose that ultimately leads to the Promise. Uncovering the fullness of who we are and where we've come from, allows us to reap the Promise—the unique harvest that is only intended for us.

Remember my premise that anyone with a financial statement is in business? But there are all types of businesses in various stages of engagement. Once you decide to leave the financial wilderness, it becomes time to elevate the standard of business you are currently engaged in to align with the legacy you desire to leave and the wealth you desire to create. Welcome to your mission. Later you will learn how you are necessary, talented, and needed.

Once the *business of you* mission is determined, you are ready for the fourth step of The NarrowRoad method: Building your wealth system to ensure you stay on The NarrowRoad. Your wealth system has been custom designed by you, and your choices include a team of people with specific resources who are as committed to building wealth your way. We will explore the key relationships you need to engage and/or develop as part of your wealth-building team. Individuals who will join your wealth journey are:

- Friends who desire similar wealth outcomes
- Family who will commit to a shared desired outcome of legacy wealth
- A financial advisor you trust
- A financial institution in whose corporate mission and vision you believe
- Messengers who speak your language about wealth creation and legacy
- An accountability network that will encourage you to stay true to the legacy you desire to lead

Wealth can be created in one generation and preserved in two. But it takes three generations to create legacy wealth, four generations to grow it, and five generations to build it. No matter what level of wealth is accomplished, it can be lost in one generation, and this is why the link must continue, and the torch must be passed.

How Do You Build Wealth?

A relationship between faith and finance is the building block of legacy wealth. In this instance, faith is complete trust or confidence in someone or something. That someone or something is entirely up to you and your theology. Finance, in this instance, is the stewardship of large amounts of capital. It's essentially the way you manage the stores of value within you; much of which is lying buried underneath the cares of the world, and your current definition of wealth creation.

Believing in something beyond yourself is essential to reach the heights that perhaps no one else in your family or community has reached before. Your relationships with what lies between your faith and your finance, once aligned with a clear vision of what wealth is for you, give you the power to build your vision of legacy wealth which is the ultimate outcome of The NarrowRoad.

Some people I interviewed associated the Promised Land with the opportunity to build a foundation for wealth creation. Few people have this perspective, and even fewer apply business and financial principles as a part of their pursuits of the Promise. As a result, the continuance of legacy wealth often gets lost in the financial wilderness due to a lack of understanding and a lack of faith in the importance of business and financial acumen. Essentially, knowing how you go about your business is crucial to building wealth.

A lifetime of work, play, love, and faith takes time and money to pursue, yet few people I interviewed felt confident about their understanding of the role of finance in wealth building. The book of Proverbs 24:3–4 states that it is wisdom that builds the house, but it is understanding through which it is established and made secure. Knowledge is what fills its rooms with rare and beautiful treasures—not surplus items from your local discount store. Knowing yourself, the choices unique to you, and the cost-benefit of each are steps to building your house the way you see it.

Step One: Creator

Every wealth journey begins with the role of the truncated middleman. The middleman is a term used to describe a journey of owning your way toward the success of your choosing. It was penned by Booker T. Washington and is necessary for everyone to master. Dr. Johnathan Sibly Butler describes the truncated middleman in his amazing book *Entrepreneurship and Self-Help Among African-Americans: A Reconsideration of Race and Economics*, "creates opportunities from despair at a time when Afro Americans were legally excluded from the opportunity structure in the nation." According to Butler, a creator of wealth along The NarrowRoad is one who: (1) adjusts to hostility by turning inward and developing economic, and community institutions (starting with their own); (2) develops a strong tradition of family stability, and excellent quality of life through housing, healthcare, and other basic forms of financial security; (3) begins a very strong emphasis on the importance of higher education for their offspring. These values are then passed down through generations. The middleman creates a foundation where there presently isn't one, through the hard work, and determination to work hard, to create a life to get ahead. Income is fuel for the fire of your torch, the seed of your legacy-wealth business. The lesson of work and finding the gift that makes room for you is the key to this first step along the road to wealth. Working hard to get ahead in life is a right everyone can use to create (financial) wealth for others and necessary income for themselves. It is the beginning of your journey to wealth when you use the skills you have to create the foundation for the life you desire. Booker T. Washington was a leader with a perspective that narrowed to the immediate concerns of his community. It was a path he viewed that would yield much promise across generations. His perspective, inherited from being the first generation in his family to navigate beyond slavery to freedom and education, was a driving force for much of the entrepreneurial endeavors of his day and today. Booker T. Washington, a fellow Hampton graduate, believed this was the path beyond the fight to a win that would fuel the exit of his community out of the storm in the financial wilderness.

Step Two: Builder

The next step along the journey to wealth is where things start to get interesting. This is what I call the first degree of freedom. There are degrees of freedom in America, meaning the "99 percent" (ignoring the mega-rich one percent of the population) are not all on the same level. The first degree of freedom, "Middle-class 101," is often one generation from survival.

With the blessing of consistent income and the use of leverage, you can arrive at a place of comfort. Your lifestyle is beginning to take shape, and some of your desires are being met. The lesson of cash flow is the gauge of the first degree of freedom.

The middle-class is what I call "talented." They know how to use leverage, savings, and investments to build a life they desire. Learning the requirements of being talented comes best from another torchbearer along The NarrowRoad, W. E. B. Du Bois.

William Edward Burghardt Du Bois (February 23, 1868–August 27, 1963) was an American civil rights activist, leader, Pan-Africanist, sociologist, educator, historian, writer, editor, poet, and scholar. After graduating from Harvard, the first African-American to earn a doctorate, he became a history, sociology, and economics professor at Atlanta University. In 1909, Du Bois was one of the co-founders of the National Association for the Advancement of Colored People (NAACP).

In September 1903, Dr. Du Bois wrote an essay titled "The Talented Tenth." The essay explained his beliefs of how his community, similar to the plight of other races, was to progress further down the road.

"The Negro race, like all races, is going to be saved by its exceptional men. The problem of education, then, among Negroes must first of all deal with the Talented Tenth; it is a problem of developing the Best of this race that they may guide the Mass away from the contamination and death of the Worst, in their own and other races."

Dr. Du Bois believed it would take a group of exceptionally educated men (and I believe, women) to lead their community to the goals he felt all communities sought to move further down the road. In The Talented Tenth, Dr. Du Bois wrote:

Its technique is a matter for educational experts, but its object is for the vision of seers. If we make money the object of man-training, we shall develop money-makers but not necessarily men; if we make technical skill the object of education, we may possess artisans but not, in nature, men. Men we shall have only as we make manhood the object of the work of the schools–intelligence, broad sympathy, knowledge of the world that was and is, and of the relation of men to it–this is the curriculum of that Higher Education which must underlie true life. On this foundation, we may build bread winning, skill of hand and quickness of brain, with never a fear lest the child and man mistake the means of living for the object of life.

As one of the highest academically trained thought leaders in his community, Dr. Du Bois realized that knowledge of money, skill, or method would not address the growing problem in his community. Rather it was wisdom, knowledge, and understanding coupled with compassion and connectedness to each other. These things were needed for the whole community to move forward towards its promise. It was not just the talented tenth who was to get ahead, but also the 90th (as I call them) were needed for the plan to succeed. Wealth is, after all, a group process.

"If this is true–and who can deny it–three tasks lay before me; first to show from the past that the Talented Tenth as they have risen among American Negroes have been worthy of leadership; secondly to show how these men may be educated and developed, and thirdly to show their relation to the Negro problem."

In picking up this great man's torch, I see within his method a similarity to what is needed today in rebuilding our communities. We need a relationship with the past narratives that serve as models for similar problems we face in our life journeys and culturally relevant curricula for everyone to use their talents to elevate the standard of business in the community. Looking at the problems in our communities as business opportunities will move us farther down the road. We are all connected, and building the life desired is partly connected with the inherited group process. Using your talents and learning from the talents of others is how you build a life for yourself and elevate the standard of business in your community.

"You misjudge us because you do not know us. From the very first, it has been the educated and intelligent of the Negro people who have led and elevated the mass..."

W.E.B. Du Bois

Along The NarrowRoad, you will find that black and white don't matter if you understand green. Creating and building the life and communities we desire requires exchanges of talents and expertise from various sources. Build what you desire with the talents in your portfolio and that of others, and you'll find that beyond the Lifestyle Journey is a pursuit of independence.

On this journey, learning to balance the present and the future is key to getting further down the road beyond lifestyle. Economies of scale stabilize the ability to live as desired. As a builder, your steps forward rely on your ability to exchange with others. Your builder step also requires emotional maturity. This allows you to establish a better relationship with money by acknowledging that everyone needs support to be the best they can be. As you will find along the road, there will be many reasons to protest and fight in the quest for freedom. It's the first degree of freedom. Remember, however, that when fighting, you'll often have very little time and or energy for anything else. Once those obstacles have been overcome, you must continue further down your NarrowRoad to build legacy wealth.

Step 3: Grower

The next step along the journey is that of the grower. This step is where you'll learn how to multiply your talents and increase the capital(s) within your wealth portfolio. This is the second degree of earned freedom, a highly productive state. By now, you've adopted and mastered the steps before and can afford to do what you want, and what you desire. In the financial wilderness, growers confidently plant their talents in various terrains, and can afford to give the time necessary to nurture low-hanging fruit, and other opportunities that take more time to come to fruition.

This second degree of freedom is often realized three generations from survival. Not only do people with this degree of freedom tend to be middle-class and middle-aged, but they also know how to increase (grow) their financial independence by partnering with the middle road. The middle road was a concept created by yet another torchbearer along The NarrowRoad, Kelly Miller (1863–1939). A prominent mathematician, sociologist, essayist, newspaper columnist, author and first African-American to attend the Ph.D. program at Johns Hopkins. He graduated from Howard Law School and became the dean of the College of Arts and Sciences. Miller modernized the classical curriculum and added new courses in the areas of natural and social sciences. An avid writer and editor who edited Booker T. Washington's and W. E. B. Du Bois works did not entirely agree with either man's philosophy that deciding a "middle road" was the best route for the black community to take to freedom. The concept of the middle road of both study and work uses the capitalist system to move people forward and includes both education and vocation.

Kelly Miller's life demonstrated how to work with perspectives not entirely agreed with when shared desire is the outcome. All three men (Washington, Du Bois, Miller) desired their communities to obtain freedom. When fused, these three legacies create an effective system of exchange—starting with ourselves, our communities, and the world. I find Miller's theory as relevant today as it was during his time.

Along The NarrowRoad is where you build your life system—one that speaks life to your unique values and needs for the degree of freedom you desire. Your life system supports your purpose, enlightens your big idea, and ensures that others understand your chosen strategic advantage to get out of the wilderness. It helps you win your battles and focuses your path to take possession of your Promised Land.

At this grower stage, ownership is the key. Your grower step relies on your ability to partner with opportunities (e.g., what you are knowledgeable of and confident in pursuing).

Step 4: Expander

The next step along the journey is that of the expander. This is the step where you are upper-middle-class with a rare degree of freedom and often four generations away from survival. Expanders have traditions and financial rituals that have spanned generations. Expanders have long seen the value in those journeying behind them and are capable of investing in their progress to further expand their legacy with compassion.

The requirements of being an expander are revealed in the legacy of yet another torchbearer who had traveled The NarrowRoad—NAACP attorney, Thurgood Marshall. His dream was to level the playing field for African-Americans. To reach financial emancipation, Marshall's idea was to plant "seed cases," which in this instance were the eleven lawsuits he filed on behalf of African-American children in the South and the District of Columbia.

Five of these cases (from South Carolina, Virginia, Delaware, Washington DC, and Kansas) finally arrived at the Supreme Court in 1952; all under the heading of Brown v. Board of Education. Marshall had what might seem to be an extremely simple view of the Reconstruction Amendments (the Thirteenth, Fourteenth, and Fifteenth) designed to secure racial equality.

Your expander step relies on your ability to invest what you see in the lives of others through your number-one quadrant—vision. Expanders create the blueprints that others will follow and benefit from for generations. Expanders leave legacies that show the cultural advantage of getting further down the road together by building and growing with other generations. Everyone can leave an unseen blueprint of the road to wealth by just modeling the road they chose to travel. Leaving a legacy narrative that truthfully reveals what is required to take the road less traveled enables the blind to see, the confused to learn, the momentum to take a quantum leap, and the mute to find their reason to speak. Take the time to find the expander in you; the world needs to benefit from your perspective.

Our Collective Journey

In what phase of the journey did you grow up? Were you raised in a middle-class household? If middle class, which degree? Can you see your life journey elevating the standard of legacy to the next degree of freedom? I hope so. Using your NarrowRoad identity and success systems, you can design a pursuit to take the legacy to the promise you desire. All you have to do is believe.

Reviewing Your Functions and Roles Along The NarrowRoad

The following questions will help you better understand The NarrowRoad you're traveling. Answer as honestly as you can. If you're honest with yourself, your road will narrow to a path conducive to your success. There are no right or wrong answers, even if they don't match everything you've read in this book—remember, for legacy wealth to be attainable, it must be defined by you and the choices you understand.

Explain your choice of description:

_____

_____

1: Describe the freedoms you feel you have in your present life experiences:

_____

_____

2: Describe the road you have selected to migrate to improve your current situation:

_____

_____

3: Describe the migration you are presently pursuing:

_____

_____

4: How far down the road do you intend to travel with the business of you—freedom, growth, or expansion?

_____

_____

5: What areas do you need help with to get to the next degree of freedom?

_____

_____

My research uncovered three roadblocks common in just about everyone's pursuit. At the end of each interview, I would share that my ultimate desired outcome for The NarrowRoad implementation is legacy wealth. The responses I would initially get were always the same. "That will never happen." "We won't work together." "No one is going to be open and honest about their money." Or, "Wealth is not for everybody."

Anchoring to an outcome you desire also makes it easier to navigate the financial wilderness of life. Life is all about stewardship—stewardship of your time, talent, and treasure in ways that multiply opportunities to grow. Stewardship in finance is wise management of the vast amounts of capital you possess and have access to, which goes beyond money. When you look at your life as a whole, you go from your father's seed, harvested by your mother, and at birth, you became invested in your family business. You are then charged with becoming a wealth creator for your lineage and others throughout your career. Along the way to becoming a creator of wealth for yourself and others, you arrive at a place where you are ready to be an investor for future generations.

With talent and capital, we are all servants of the continuum, but many bury these talents in the sands of illiteracy, confusion, chaos, and doubt. If you are reading this book, it's time to master the art of your business so that individually and collectively, you can create a life of purpose and promise. Imagine, if the average career span is forty years, we can all be million-dollar businesses in our unique ways.

The journey to the Promised Land is a familiar narrative that we know shines a light on the reality of a purpose-driven life. A promise is something each member of the link must pursue and take possession of. We must believe that the time and risks involved in pursuing unlimited wealth are worth it. It's time to find your group, exchange within it, and build your wealth. Growth and expansion align with the choices we make and the risks we take.

Fear, chaos, confusion, and doubt leave many promises buried in the sands of history. But a promise is forever, and all one has to do is connect, anchor, remember, believe, and pursue. So, let's take some time to find the necessary elements to once again believe in promises.

The years of my Jolly-Journey have given me extreme insight into the various relationships with money that exist in our communities and households. I gained most of my insight from the data I collected during a national assessment survey of faith and finance to support the creation of The NarrowRoad, and my doctoral research. I talked to more than seventy thousand people about their relationship with money, ownership, business, and desires for legacy wealth. I studied the patterns, and created a series of algorithms to lead others out of the financial wilderness and onto the road toward wealth creation. I tested my findings with thousands of people in seminars, lectures, classes, and church groups and have been sharing my understanding of the importance of legacy wealth across the country ever since.

Along the journey, so many people would respond in disbelief to my question, "Do you share your financial goals with those you love?"

They often say, "Share my financial goals and objectives with friends and family? What? I could never do that!"

Why not? I ask them.

Responses included:

I am a private person!

I don't like talking about money!

They might share my plan with others!

Nobody sees things the way I do about money!

I just feel uncomfortable doing that!

To that, I say...hmmm. My research and studies have shown that there can be little to no meaningful exchange without trust in a relationship. The biggest obstacle to working together in a community is often trust. Groups with the best intentions often hit roadblocks when trusting one another with key things like money, the responsibility to plan things, the ability to execute, or the capacity to deliver. These choices leave us in the storm of doing everything ourselves.

Building wealth our way is culturally influenced. We know this. In many communities, people are doing six jobs but are only getting paid for the one they are most talented in, and that income is all that is available to them to build into real income. But wealth is not created in isolation. If we understood wealth as a group process, most of us might not try to do everything ourselves. Taking on the full burden of earning income, spending it, trying to sow something of value, and passing that value on to the next generation with the hopes that they will do the same, might not be so overwhelming. Anyone trying to do all these things alone is in, what I call, the storm. The storm is when you carry the load of everything.

Wealth has a language of its own, with definitions that are shared, trusted, and of course, understood. To get there, you must develop a comfort level talking about money, wealth, ownership, and legacy. This is a conversation that expands beyond the hope-and-dream state. This is not a brainstorming of what could be. This is a sharing of what will be, and that is where wealth begins.

What I found in my research is that lack of trust is a symptom of something deeper—a lack of organization. In many cases, we are not structured in our financial matters, which leads to a misunderstanding of what is valuable independently, and what is more valuable when shared. I, for one, was raised with the belief that you can't lose something God gave you, yet we are tight-lipped when it comes to wealth and legacy. As a result, our elders can tell us what to do but not how to do it, which often leaves us wandering in the storm of financial wilderness during the prime years of our window of opportunity to build wealth. Mutual funds, the stock market, living trusts, and wills require groups to plan and execute.

The storm that lives in the financial wilderness is why some inherit property and resources, and then spend years afraid to touch them because they don't know how to discuss what to do with their siblings. The storm is why some work hard all their lives and have little to show for it when it comes to retirement.

Yet the simple principles of time, the value of money, and compound interest reveal that the sooner we engage our window of opportunity from a legacy perspective, the more time we have to build and grow the wealth we most desire. With structure, we become organized; and with organization, we become clearer about what needs to be shared to multiply.

I also found that the lack of organization around the possessions and experiences we value, when commingled with society's definition of what's important, led us to hold on to everything from the fear of risking or losing anything. What we lacked was a roadmap, a system to navigate both the risk and return of exchanging things of value for what is most valuable to our desired standard of living.

Things You Need to Build Wealth

Systems are key to building wealth your way. Your NarrowRoad ID reveals many things, including the key elements required for your wealth-building process. Everyone along The NarrowRoad has a weakness that needs structure—something they struggle with when trying to do it alone. Consider the role in your fourth quadrant, your perceived weakness, that when supported by others, becomes your most innate strength. It is the root of your purpose. Want a key to building wealth your way? Ask for support with either your vision, thought, action, or emotional processes and watch how the impossible becomes possible to build wealth your way. See the chart below to determine which key is yours to get past what blocks you.

Wealth Needs		
Models	A model that aligns with your vision of wealth and shows a clear path to get there.	☐
Strategies	A proven method or process that educates and helps you facilitate key wealth decisions.	☐
Structure	A tactical, practical system that advises you and holds you accountable.	☐
Engagement	A group to share and pursue ideas and plans with.	☐

Who Is Part of Your Wealth Group?

Think of the wealth group process as a value chain, where each link is integral to getting further down the road toward your desired destination. However far you are willing to take it, the first link in the value chain is your vision. Taking the time to reflect on your past, present, and desired future is the first step to building a wealth group process. There is a statistic that says your net worth is the average of your five closest friends. Think about your core group of friends. Is this true for you?

When I shared this concept of the group process, many people who saw wealth as an important outcome to reach asked this question, "But what about my childhood friends who did not choose the paths I chose?" It's a valid question and one that keeps many families and friends stuck in the relationship's avoidance zone.

I have a dear friend and her husband who chose to send their daughter to private school. They decided to assist the parents of their daughter's closest friend with tuition so that their daughter's best friend could attend the same school. They had good jobs, but they had a different outlook on the value of their finances. I asked my friend if she and her husband ever considered talking to them about the wealth choices they had made to prepare for their children's future and retirement. My friend had invested early in property and had put money aside for both children's college education. They lived comfortably and looked at their household as a business with various streams of income. They shared investments across generations and other groups of friends. They had their group process down, yet they were still anxious about having the conversation with someone whose values were different but who could use a straightforward conversation and tangible proof of what is possible.

Your wealth group must include professionals—legal, tax, and financial advisors. It must also include family across generations—parents, grandparents, cousins, nieces, nephews and it further expands when you can include friends. The next step is to expand the legacy beyond those with the degrees, access, and know-how to help implement the ideas and dreams you envision. Many have the will to do so if only an invitation were extended to join a group focused on defining and achieving wealth and sharing knowledge and experience beneficial for their next leg of the road.

The Wealth Journey Continues

Like the Israelites, many who sought freedom often failed to take full possession of inheritances. For example, today's wealthiest segment in the African-American community is my grandparents' generation. Now between their late seventies and nineties, that generation (often born of sharecroppers) journeyed, marched, protested, and fought for the right to take possession of their freedom. For them, freedom was ownership. Yet many in that wealthy generation do not have trusts, wills or systems to pass on an inheritance. My parent's generation's beneficiaries are often asset rich but cash poor, which reduces their ability to buy their hard-earned assets out of probate, when left unprotected, to pass on to the next generation. Probate is a system of administering the estate of a deceased person that resolves all claims and ensures the distribution of the deceased person's property under a will. Ownership includes integrating systems of independence with systems of accountability. For many, there is a break across these systems, which leads to a loss of hard-earned wealth. There is a valid historical context for this distrust in the African-American community.

The Freedman's Bank, formed as a savings and wealth-building tool for enslaved people, robbed black people at all socioeconomic levels of their life savings when the bank, managed by an all-white board of directors, failed. Unlike other banks, the FIDC failed to protect the depositors. Black bank customers lost over 57 million in deposits. The same lack of accountability occurred in 1920 in Tulsa, Oklahoma, when a thriving black community was burned to the ground by whites. As much distrust as this caused, to move forward to the promise, our grasshopper mentality needs to be overcome and replaced by well-thought-out strategies to remove obstacles blocking the path to the Promised Land. A "grasshopper mentality" (see Numbers 13:33 King James Version) is when faced with the giant decision of whether legacy will be a wealth-creating business of permanence, or a talent buried in the sand of legality, results in three generations of owners failing to leave equity on the table, for the next generation's advancement toward freedom. Equity is a form of wealth that too few understand, so when wealth is delayed for another forty years, the wandering cycle in the wilderness begins again.

What Does Wealth Mean to You?

In your lifetime, will you attain it? What is your relationship between faith and finance? What torch have you picked up to carry further down the road of freedom? As a country, to get to the promised land, despite many arguments and disagreements, we must collectively answer a few questions and address many concerns. As I learned from Dr. Shawn Copeland while in seminary, an argument is not a fight, it is a means to make something clear.

The Wealth Argument: Can we collectively get out of the financial wilderness? A country of our size and first-world leadership could be a model of collective wealth for all citizens.

The Wealth Problem: For most families and communities, the journey to legacy wealth is uncharted territory. Without a shared system for navigating the road to wealth in ways we can understand, how will we find an inclusive solution for all families?

The Burning Wealth Question: Can individuals form wealth groups to cooperatively learn and build, grow and expand wealth that passes on for generations?

The Convincing Wealth Data: For many in America, business and finance are things to be avoided and to mistrust, yet for wealth builders, they are the keys to designing a path toward multigenerational wealth creation and preservation.

Building wealth is a long-term choice hidden amongst many short-term options that skip the necessary steps required for wealth building. Each individual can build personal wealth, with their primary assets being their time, talent, and legacy perspective.

Personal wealth can lead to collective wealth, which can be used to support the needs of others. Businesses solve problems, and with so many problems in our communities, an ever-growing national debt, and city and state budgets failing, now is the time for more to understand how wealth and business are related and can be used to improve the world in which we live.

The Persuasive Wealth Message: Legacy wealth is an inter-generational process of collective agreement and strategy. Commitment to the collective agreement must be renewed with each generation for it to continue in its development.

The Persuasive Wealth Solution: Legacy wealth is a group process that can be created in three generations. The intergenerational wealth system must be embraced as a group agreement and anchored to principles that reflect the unique legacy perspectives represented in the group.

The Negotiating Wealth Practice: Legacy wealth building is possible when using financial and business acumen to navigate beyond one's current financial situation, to chart a path that successfully leads to legacy wealth. An integrating strategy that includes individual and collective goals and objectives are, in practice, both qualitative and quantitative.

The Wealth invitation: Our journey together through The NarrowRoad Guide is in understanding a shared-legacy perspective that can unite us and hasten our departure from the financial wilderness and toward legacy wealth creation.

Chapter Thirteen

JOURNEYING BEYOND THE NARROWROAD... TO EMANCIPATION

The choice to journey beyond a road that is often blocked by race, gender, creed, confusion around class, and privilege requires the realization that the shared life we are all living is still in many ways based on a plantation business model. While we live in different sections of the plantation, we are all in one way or another under its oppressive rule. This is killing the generational promise of wealth as a legacy. Every fourth generation repeats itself, providing the opportunity for us all to learn from our individual and collective pursuits, and turn the wheel further down the road. Together, once liberated, we can pursue shared equity and the fulfillment of the promise. We all have inherited a seat at the equity table, and, from my perspective, we are closer than we think to elevating our standard of business to include the promises and expectations written as a vision 246 years ago.

Often, impassioned and forceful words precede the exodus from slavery to poverty and from emancipation to emerging freedom. Often, death precedes the second exodus toward freedom. Going from fear of the full responsibility of what freedom means requires sacrifice and unblinded faith that the inherited ownership and the wealth of the promise will ensue.

Elements of promises realized remain consistent across journeys I have observed. Ranging from the colonization of America to the pursuit of freedom post-slavery, these journeys all resulted in a migration of some kind. This delay causes one generation to wander and die as another commits to stop wandering, and the journey continues its patterned circle. To acquire a successful leadership role, to fight battles, win victories, and take possession of Promise, a leap of faith is needed. It is time we unblind it.

The Genesis of America—A Land Without Promise (Yet).

In its beginning, America, often thought of as the land of milk and honey, was anything but. Most of its first settlers died from starvation. It took seven long years of repeated failure for the first displaced group to build a land of free enterprise in Jamestown, Virginia, to succeed. The early settlers were forced to leave what was familiar and envisioned starting a new business venture to build wealth from mining gold; that was their plan. Armed with the history that colonization was nothing new to English settlers, it was believed that America would be no different than simply taking possession of a colony. However, in the early 1600s, the periods of starvation kept killing each new group of determined settlers. In Jamestown, the creature comforts of organization, policy, and free labor—otherwise known as slavery—had yet to be established.

Leadership, tools to build a nation, and resources to feed the first movers, were common issues in the wilderness of early America. Before it became united, America began with a centralized collective model to navigate out of the wilderness, believing that they would have enough to succeed if they pulled from one storehouse. Unlike the Israelites, whose supply came from God, the early American settlers were expected to replenish the storehouse from the harvest produced from their work on the land. America's genesis would not yield its intended promise without challenges and failure. Many of the first immigrants died trying to create a life. Over time, successful colonies were established by the next generation, who had adopted a shared system of slavery to build it.

A Dream Deferred—Hopes and Dreams Migrate Through Ways and Means

What happens to a dream deferred? It becomes a torch waiting to be found, picked up, or passed on to the next generation. Every generation has the audacity to hope their dream will come true one day. The reality is that very few live to see it in its entirety. Your hope needs a plan, and your dream needs a mission, and both need ways and means to bring it to fruition. One lifetime is seldom long enough.

There is always a lot of work to do when journeying in both the financial wilderness and in the pursuit of the Promised Land. No one can do it alone. While your tribe working together can accomplish a dimension of the outcome, there is always an opportunity for those who have inherited a different perspective and set of skills to fill the blind spots. The work enables each generation to reap the inherited harvests that lead to increased opportunities to pursue the promise and the means to sustain it. Along The

NarrowRoad, each generation has an inherited win, and a unique job to do while working to exit the financial wilderness. Finding the way to finish this generational mission is the collective journey along a road narrowed by individual and collective choices.

The Israelites wilderness experience is a model for organizing according to skill and tribal assignment. Their wilderness was organized into four standards (lion, man, ox, eagle). Each standard contained three tribes and one group within the Levites. The centermost tribe, the tribe of Levi, was divided into four sub-groups, one sub-group for each standard. The tribe of Levi was the only tribe that did not receive a direct land inheritance within the Promised Land. That was because their responsibility to God was too great to add the burden of the other Israelites responsibilities. Do you have within your social circle those friends and family members who, no matter what, choose to focus on the greater good before the good of themselves? These individuals are always in the middle of things, wanting more for the collective than they do for themselves, and are willing to risk it all to do it.

The Levi tribe's responsibility became one of moving ahead to maintain the construction and breakdown of the tent that held the Arc of the Covenant, the central tent of witness. The Arc of the Covenant always sat in the center of the camp during the wandering in the wilderness. When the time came to leave the wilderness, the Levi's were the first to enter Jordan, and as a result, the promised land; followed by the lion, man, ox, and eagle standards. My grandmother would always caution me to do things "in decency and order." She would say it was important to "begin like you were going to end." The order of things mattered for the Israelites in their journey through the wilderness and into their inherited land of promise. Order matters a lot to your journey to pursue your dreams with the ways and means required to fulfill them.

Once the framework for America was established, it worked similarly to the wilderness operations in the biblical promised land narrative. There was an escape from slavery that led to a wilderness in search of opportunity but without an equitable plan for progress that included everyone. Emancipation, as a result, scattered former enslaved Africans to the four corners of our evolving nation. For Africans, sharecropping was the initial business model to pursue freedom. This path along the road to wealth was filled with hard work and a lot of hope. When threats to this break-even existence persisted, a second move emerged—the great migration. This strategy came with expectations that the hopes and deferred dreams of inclusion would be realized. These two strategies, the first move of hard work, and the second move of migrating for greater opportunity, with the hopes and dreams of arriving at the cross-generational pursuit of inherited promises, goes on to this day. The ways and means for taking possession of the promise are baked into the best intentions and a bevy of blind faith.

In the American Promised Land narrative, however, the enslaved Africans were tasked with building up and tearing down the plantation fields in times of seed, planting, and harvest. This segment of the American business model staff did not receive an inherited portion at harvest time. Their sweat equity passed on in deferred dreams. Unlike the Levites, persons enslaved in America were not acknowledged for their role in successfully helping to navigate America out of the wilderness and into the promised land position of a superpower. Formerly enslaved people were left with broken promises, even though by 1860, there were more millionaires per capita in the Mississippi Valley than anywhere else in the United States, thanks to their free labor.

Wherever you go, you take your wealth with(in) you.

I found in my research that history repeats itself. Understanding your history, as a result, can become a predictive model of sorts to guide you in the ways you are to go, with the means you are earning and have inherited.

> "Slaves' humanity was not restricted to a zone of agency or culture outside their work. When slaves went into the field, they took with them social connections and affective ties. The labor process flowed through them, encompassed them, and was interrupted and redefined by them. Slaves worked alongside people they knew, people they had raised, and people they would bury. They talked, they sang, they laughed, they suffered, they remembered their ancestors and their God; the rhythms of their lives working through and over those of their work. We can no more separate the labor of slaves from their humanity, than we can separate the ability of a human hand to pick cotton. Nor can we separate their ability to caress the cheek of a crying child, rub the aching stooped back from the arc of a body bent in supplication, or the voice that called time for the hoes striking the ground; that which told a story, centuries old." [2]

The slave narratives above reveal that throughout America, slaves in faith sought out God's witness and protection as they toiled the land of their "masters." Believing that as they worked to reap harvests that would finance the building of the world's fastest-growing superpower, one day, they too, like their

---

[2] River of Dark Dreams, Walter Johnson

masters, would inherit their Promised Land. Think about your current journey to wealth; Where are you blind to how or when the outcome you seek will manifest? What keeps you moving forward despite the lack of clear vision?

For America's first asset, the formal invitation to believe in the Promise came some 150 years ago in the form of emancipation. Preceding emancipation was a civil war that slaves themselves supported and fought for in exchange for their Promise. Once the "Red Sea" of the civil war was crossed, exodus into the financial wilderness was a reality that took generations to navigate after various attempts to possess the land. Generation after generation of this population of Americans migrated into the four winds, choosing to migrate to North, Deeper South, East and West, seeking ways and means to transition from being a creator of wealth for the nation to a wealth creator for themselves.

The Emancipation Proclamation was an executive order issued by President Abraham Lincoln to all segments of the Executive branch of the United States on January 1, 1863; as a war measure during the American Civil War. It proclaimed the freedom of 3.1 million of the 4 million slaves in the United States in the ten states still in rebellion. The Proclamation was based on the president's constitutional authority as commander in chief of the armed forces; it was not a law passed by Congress. The Proclamation did not compensate the owners, nor did it outlaw slavery, and it certainly did not make the ex-slaves (called *freedmen*) citizens. What it did was to make the eradication of slavery an explicit war goal, in addition to the goal of reuniting the Union.

Eighty-five years later, in July 1948, President Harry S. Truman signed Executive Order 9981, which in theory declared "that there shall be equality of treatment and opportunity for all persons in the armed services without regard to race, color, religion, or national origin."

The march for the Promise began. A key marker in the Civil Rights movement is the historic Brown v. Board of Education verdict won by unanimous agreement in 1954 by NAACP attorney Thurgood Marshall. Support came from Pauli Murray, the first black person to earn a Doctor of the Science of Law from Yale. She was also founder of the National Organization of Women and it was her brilliant legal arguments and constitutional interpretations that were winning strategies for public school desegregation. The victory declared segregation in public schools unconstitutional. This ruling, a first step in legally defining the bridge to independence via equality, paved the way for large-scale desegregation. Marshall saw his dream, to level the playing field, in motion. To get to even more emancipation, Thurgood's idea was to plant "seed cases," which in this case were the eleven lawsuits he filed on behalf of African-American children in the South and the District of Columbia.

"Five of these cases—from South Carolina; Virginia; Delaware; Washington DC; and Kansas—finally arrived at the Supreme Court in 1952 under the heading of Brown." Marshall had what might seem to be an extremely simple view of the Reconstruction Amendments—the 13th, 14th and 15th Amendments—designed to secure racial equality. Let that equality begin.

A year later, in 1955, in Montgomery, Alabama, Rosa Parks ignited a second step toward independence by refusing to give up her seat at the front of the "colored section" of a bus to a white passenger. Her action defied a southern custom of the time. In response to her arrest, the Montgomery black community launched a yearlong bus boycott that forced the city to desegregate the buses on December 21, 1956. This victory is the spark that ignites the flame of Reverend Martin Luther

King Jr., a new minister in the area who would quickly ascend to become a leader of the movement along a different road toward the same promise.

In 1963 more than two hundred thousand people joined the March on Washington, where participants from around the world would listen to the now-famous "I Have a Dream" speech, very little of which was written on paper.

Almost a year later, President Johnson signed the *Civil Rights Act of 1964*. "The most sweeping civil rights legislation since Reconstruction" prohibiting discrimination of all kinds based on race, color, religion, or national origin. Unlike Brown v. Board of Education, this law also provided the federal government with the powers to enforce desegregation. The walls of Jericho had started to come crumbling down.

The late 1960s also had its fair share of dark places. In February 1965, Malcolm X, the black nationalist and founder of the Organization of Afro-American Unity, was shot to death presumably by members of the *Black Muslim* faith, which Malcolm had recently left in favor of orthodox Islam. Similar to the battle of Ai (Joshua 8:1–35), the Nation of Islam, in their quest for change, had divisions within. The patterns of history continue to repeat themselves.

A month later, in Selma, Alabama, a march in support of voting rights is stopped at the Pettus Bridge by a police blockade. The incident is dubbed Bloody Sunday by the media as fifty marchers were hospitalized due to police brutality. This march is considered the catalyst for pushing through the voting rights act five months later, on August 10, 1965. This Act made it easier for southern African-Americans to register to vote. The voice of an oppressed people was beginning to be heard.

The year 1968 marks the battle that brought the fire and the pain. On April 4th, hours after he'd preached that he had been to the mountaintop, thirty-nine-year-old Rev. Dr. Martin Luther King, Jr. was shot and killed as he stood on the balcony outside his hotel room. President Johnson signed the Civil Rights Act days later prohibiting discrimination in the sale, rental, and financing of housing. America legally opened the gates to the full Promise of our land but emotionally backpedaled as barrier laws were put in place with slow-moving social acceptance and enforcement.

For African-Americans, the transition to becoming wealth creators for themselves is indeed a multigenerational lesson in business and finance that impacts the entire nation, if not the world. The historical journey of the Africans to becoming African-American demonstrates the elements of The Narrow-Road method for legacy wealth. African-American legacy goes back a couple of years from slavery in the legacy narratives of people who decided to take their life, liberty and pursuit personally before laws and policies were firmly established.

The thoughts and dreams of Frederick Douglass, Harriet Tubman, Mary McCloud Bethune, and Reginald Lewis demonstrate how one must learn when best to pursue actions that create both life for yourself and progress for others is in our shared history. The lived and spoken messages of Sojourner Truth, Ida B. Wells, Dr. King, Malcolm X and Thurgood Marshall spoke to the joy and pain of staying connected to things that matter and that all lead to outcomes that create, build, grow, and expand what the business of living is all about.

The pursuit of promise has many dimensions. At its core is the wealth passed on by remembering. Take some time to connect the dots in your part of the wilderness, to look back down the road you are traveling, and I promise you will find a glimpse of light in whatever dark place you find yourself. There is nothing new under the sun. Which turn of the Wealth Wheelhas been left up to you? If you take time to look, every fourth generation repeats itself. Which turn of the wealth wheel has been left up to you.

Along The NarrowRoad it is your vision that leads to thoughts about "how," which leads to actions of "what" and messages of "why." These internal steps result in external outcomes of great value over time, anchoring us to incremental pursuits of progress that raise our standards of living, expectations, and accomplishments. The visionaries, thinkers, doers, and speakers alive in your friends and family network consciously and unconsciously live lives that connect across history to create a legacy passed on for generations. Wealth is created when you build on lessons learned from a shared history that is remembered and learned. What about our history enables you to move further in your life pursuit? What makes you proud can make you even more determined to ensure the wheel of wealth continues to progress further down the road.

When the legacy connection to our life pursuits is forgotten, the opportunity for wealth creation is not passed on to the next generation. It is stored up like a hidden treasure waiting for someone to remember the legacy. The cycle begins again from the beginning—such as a fight for education, equality, and laws that support the winning of battles fought and won before and are waiting to be reborn in a memory.

It is for these reasons The NarrowRoad is a guide for elevation and liberation.

- Elevating our history to the guidepost can liberate the confused mind about what it takes to make the impossible possible.

- Elevating our legacy to wealth to liberate the perspective that struggles, in the same way, is a part of the inherited promise.

- Elevating our pursuit of happiness to ownership to liberate the belief that income and wealth are the same.
- Elevating our journey to life purpose to liberate each generation to pursue their own vision for wealth supported in part by an inherited perspective.

We are born into an ongoing legacy narrative, and we make it what we choose to remember and build upon. It's a series of unconscious and conscious choices that become our dialog with ourselves, our community, and our world. Our history is a roadmap of what is possible when an idea evolves into a dream, becomes a mission, and builds into a shared system—a way of life that becomes the vision for the future to expand with their inherited perspective of what is possible. It is in this way that history becomes prophecy. The pattern continues when the roles people play pass from one generation to the next—and Moses becomes Joshua, Dr. King becomes President Obama, Michael Jordan becomes Kobe Bryant, and Shirley Chisholm becomes Hillary Clinton, and Hillary Clinton becomes Kamala Harris.

Your idea becomes your granddaughter's vision and your great granddaughter's reality. This pattern of progress spares no one and offers the invitation to contribute where you see fit to keep the wheel of progress turning. All you have to do is stay connected. Connection is an interesting thing. It in itself forms a pattern within a pattern. The idea of the American Dream was improved by the aristocracy, who determined that to build America as a land of the free, you needed ownership amongst the pioneers; the right to life, liberty, and pursuit of ownership became the strategy to keep the progress wheels moving forward. Ownership requires work, and the work, in the beginning, was the mission of the slaves, who, while working for their masters, believed that, despite deplorable conditions, one day would result in their own freedom and inclusion into the business model where they were the first asset.

The work required a structure to be built and a system to scale as necessary to attain freedom as a nation and sustain it. The system builders, who structured the order of the land into the Bill of Rights and the Constitution, further moved the wheel of progress forward. Finally, the vision for one nation under God emerged after a few necessary negotiations via amendments intended to have the workers and the experts pursue the promise in this land. Still not on equal footing, the wheel continued to turn (ideas, dreams, visions, missions and systems), all leading to sharable desired outcomes. This is and continues to be our shared history.

From which turn of the wheel did you come? We did not all start in the room where deferred dreams became realities. I came from workers, mission-driven people who were determined to do for others long enough to earn the right to do for themselves. I also come from experts and masters, who, with the assistance of workers, built wealth in this land that passed on for generations. This combination of perspectives, hopes, dreams, and lived realities make me who I am today. Their lives are the base for the models of the visions we look to when reflecting on our history. When reviewing history, we often jump from idea to vision, leaving necessary elements out of the story. This leads to repetitive cycles similar to wandering in the wilderness, seeking the treasure that was lost again due to lapses in memory of the key elements of progress.

The elders reveal the hidden truth when they repeatedly say the way forward is back through. Adults reveal their order when they claim that the youth do not know how to move forward. The youth reveal their need for organization when they claim the elders do not know of what they speak. As a result, we all in some way rely on blind faith to turn these dispersed ideas into dreams, then into missions that build systems of hoped-for vision attainment.

Our history is a prophecy, and a prophecy is a vision for an appointed time. My quest with The NarrowRoad was to put the puzzle pieces together so I could cease walking blindly along the roads that had been laid before us. Once again, opening our eyes with purpose, begin our unique journey of taking our ideas to experts to convert them into dreams that'll be taken on as missions and further built upon into systems that reveal a vision whose time has finally come. There is no need to rewrite history. There is a need to unearth hidden treasure in your life so that you can pick up the torch of your legacy and move it forward to a system of wealth creation that will, over your lifetime, become a model for legacy wealth for your family and community.

Journeying beyond The NarrowRoad requires embodying the true meaning of unity as a nation. Unity leads the way to unlocking the inherited promise of the promised land—ownership for all. For America to reach her promise, your theology, in this case, liberation theology, is the key to choosing the road that few people find and even fewer take. Emancipation, without liberation as a shared belief, is freedom without a business plan, masked by a diversity and inclusion message without a strategy to implement its necessary outcome. Journeying beyond The NarrowRoad to a place where wealth is a standard, and rules and regulations are a means to more intimate (business) relationships that pursue the purpose of wealth creation that passes on for generations is the unfinished business we all must commit to finishing.

Reviewing Your Life, Liberty, and the Pursuit of Promise

The following will help you better understand The NarrowRoad you are traveling. Answer as honestly as you can. If you're honest with yourself, your road will narrow to a road most conducive to your success. There are no right or wrong answers, even if they don't match everything you've read in this book—remember, for legacy wealth to be attainable, it must be defined by you and the choices you understand.

1: The first promise along The NarrowRoad is the ability to sustain yourself with the talents you have been given. This is measured by income and your ability to afford your needs. Reflect on your current financial situation and how close you are to fulfilling this promise.

_____

_____

2: The second promise along The NarrowRoad is the ability to leverage your relationships with others to build a life you desire. This is measured by systems, groups, and structures you collaborate with to get what you want. Reflect on your current lifestyle and how close you are to fulfilling the wants you desire in your life.

_____

_____

3: The third promise along The NarrowRoad is the ability to grow your financial independence beyond those who came before you. This is measured by your partnerships, strategies to get to the next degree of freedom for yourself, and generational advancement in life compared to your parents and grandparents. Reflect on your strategies for financial independence and how confident you feel in your present pursuit.

_____

_____

4: The fourth promise along The NarrowRoad is the ability to pass on your wealth wisdom to the next generation through an investment of at least one of your five capitals. This is measured by those who pick up your torch and carry your legacy narrative forward. Reflect on the ways your leadership and vision impact those who are journeying the road behind you. What will be your legacy narrative for them?

_____

_____

5: The fifth promise along The NarrowRoad is the prayer you have for the fourth and fifth generations you will not live to see but who will benefit from the legacy of your pursuit. What is the future and hope you desire for them, and how can your faith plant a seed to carry it through?

_____

_____

6. The sixth promise along The NarrowRoad is your ability to recognize your own shackles and your ability to embrace inclusion for all citizens. Where do you stand in your opinion?

_____

_____

Chapter Fourteen

LEGACY WEALTH AT LAST: REVIEWING LESSONS LEARNED ON THE NARROWROAD—IT WILL WORK IF YOU WORK IT

The number one wealth decision is the difference between creating wealth for others and becoming a wealth creator for yourself.

Your financial decisions determine how far down the legacy wealth road you will travel. While wealth is more than money, it is important to remember a successful pursuit of wealth requires ways and means to keep up the momentum. The NarrowRoad journey is a series of four steps that create, build, grow, and expand. You have the ability, capital, and opportunity to journey down the road to wealth your way. Your NRID is what accelerates your progress once you understand and apply the knowledge of your self-worth to your process.

The first step of any journey is that of a creator of wealth. Your time spent working benefits the long-term vision of someone paying you. In exchange for your time, you get money. How you value, it is up to you, your budget and your wealth perspective. In this light, you are a creator of wealth and a generator of income for yourself. The next steps along the road reveal the different degrees of freedom necessary to balance the equation to support your wealth desires.

Wealth development is built in stages and phases—the further down the road, the more opportunities are exposed. There are many options in life, but wealth creation choices are limited to a few specific tools to build, grow, and expand the value of your holdings. The NarrowRoad teaches the principles of business and finance so that you can elevate your life to whichever degree of freedom you choose.

Legacy Wealth Migrations

The journey of America illustrates the pattern of how wealth is created from early through to the present day. Early pioneers who

Defining Progress

Along the NarrowRoad™ there are three degrees of freedom.

Each degree of freedom elevates your standard of business inviting you to a responsibility and opportunity to build wealth your way.

Steps Along The NarrowRoad

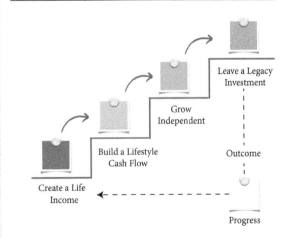

worked individually to create a better life for themselves starved to death. The second generation became the founders who joined forces to build a system that propelled America's quantum-leaps forward as a superpower. The enslaved Africans' transition from slavery to three degrees of freedom are examples of the levels of wealth creation possible along the road measured by class. Each pathway shares patterns that resemble both the narratives of the parable of the talents and the hidden treasures in the field.

As evidenced by the early American settlers, predating the Civil War and the emergent sharecroppers post-Emancipation, being the first of anything is a difficult journey. Many sacrifices were made for very little retained reward. It is always difficult to sustain oneself without an overarching vision for how things begin and end. Exit is just as important as an entry of an event. Building and growing something created is very difficult for first movers. It takes the leverage of different perspectives joining together to build traction for future momentum.

For a group, no longer stifled by the ability to use only one talent (time), for capital accumulation, freedom is a matter of ownership of one's dream; which emancipation provides the opportunity to pursue, and liberation affords the ability to possess. The degrees of freedom are pursued based on how one plans the life distance between emancipation of their time and the freedom to create income with skills, talents and abilities unique to the wealth builder who is determined to navigate on the first servant level. Emancipation is defined as the process of being set free from legal, social, or political restrictions. To fulfill the definition of emancipation, one must become liberated in vision, thought, action, speech and outcome. Emancipated slaves had the opportunity to migrate to another location or sharecrop with former plantation owners. The pursuit to do what they had done for their former masters for themselves, was often detoured due to limited resources, which led them to sell their future for the seed capital required to build some level of freedom for themselves.

While this may seem a journey that often repeats itself, it's important to note that the first and second degrees of freedom fall between the sharecropper, who did what they could with what they had, and the migrant who formed networks and groups to work independently within uncharted territory. Understanding various levels of business, and how they best operate is very important to overcoming the inherent battles of those working to make a life and leave wealth and a legacy for themselves and others.

You now know it takes three generations to build legacy wealth. One generation to work hard and create a talent (or twenty-plus years of resources). One generation can multiply these talents to build a plan for freedom, and one generation can grow these talents into a productive system of support for themselves and others. The mastery level is where anyone with a vision can participate if they understand how to pursue opportunities and invest in them. To see the value before it's created makes a master capable of reaping the harvests of seeds that they did not sow themselves.

Understanding various journeys offers the ability to see the different pathways and timeframes available to build your wealth as you've defined it. Many roads lead to one's ability to impact the future; we will come to know. All roads that have been taken here in America can enlighten us to what choices, and options we cannot afford to wait on pursuing.

In the Bible, the parable of the talents reveals the decisions and choices of four wealth builders: the master and the first, second, and third servants; all of whom worked under the master. The master had the vision. The first servant had the mind and position to learn firsthand from the master. The second servant had the relationships and ability to build from the success of the first servant. The third servant had the opportunity to be on the same road as the three others. The master was a shrewd investor and gave talents to each of the three servants according to his perspective of their abilities. A talent was roughly the equivalent of one million dollars. The master invested five talents to the first servant, two talents to the second servant, and one talent to the third servant. Before he left on a business journey, he shared one expectation: each was to be a wise steward of what the master had given them. The outcomes of each servant represent what it means to build, grow, and expand along The NarrowRoad. Both the first and second servants earned a 100% return on investment, with the first receiving a bonus for their good stewardship. The third servant chose to bury their talent in the sand for safekeeping, fearful of losing what they had been given; this was deemed a poor example of stewardship. The punishment for that decision was to be cast out, and the talent they had been given taken and reinvested with the first servant.

The legacy example of A. G. Gaston (1892–1996), an African-American millionaire who learned how to multiply his various talents, was the grandson of sharecroppers. Gaston learned from his grandmother and grandfather, former slaves who worked together post-emancipation as sharecroppers and entrepreneurs. Gaston grew up during a time that Booker T. Washington largely influenced. Washington encouraged blacks to believe in the philosophy of self-help, racial solidarity, and accommodation. Washington urged blacks to, "accept discrimination" for the time being and concentrate on elevating themselves through hard work and material prosperity. He believed in education, crafts, industrial and farming skills, and cultivating the virtues of patience, enterprise, and thrift. This, he said, would win the respect of whites and lead to African-Americans being fully accepted as citizens and integrated into all strata of society.

After serving in the military, Gaston went to work in the mines of Alabama. There he got the idea to sell lunches to the men with whom he worked. Since his mother and grandmother, who learned the skill while on the plantation, were superior cooks, he partnered with them. He established a robust business and earned quite a bit of trust from his customers. This business expanded to lending money at a 25 percent interest. Later, as mining was a dangerous business that often resulted in death, he began selling burial insurance to his coworkers. Gaston partnered with his father-in-law in the funeral business and later opened a savings bank providing banking services to his community.

Gaston is a perfect example of a second servant who worked with others to fill a need in his extended social network. He grew to that of a first servant, as his business endeavors afforded him the opportunity to build enterprises, that filled the needs of his community, and proved financially beneficial even to those outside of his community. He sold his business to his employees as his legacy, desiring to continue Booker T. Washington's legacy of self-help, hard work, and material prosperity.

Reginald Lewis (1942 – 1993) is the quintessential example of a quantum leap from a second servant to a master. The first to attend college in his family, he went to Harvard Law School after graduating from Virginia State University. In observing the world of mergers and acquisitions, Lewis quickly saw that the way to wealth creation was through acquisition. Lewis was the first African-American to buy a billion-dollar business. In his purchase, he opened the doors for employment opportunities to communities that had yet to get beyond the position of the third servant.

There are various ways to build an enterprise capable of sustaining your desired level of freedom. Knowing yourself (your strengths and weaknesses) enables you to pursue multiplying your talents at levels that enable anyone to build wealth however they define it.

The business model of slavery is beneficial as a teaching tool because it has impacted every American. Understanding how the American standard was first created, then built, grown and expanded during the 276 years America navigated before eliminating its unfair advantage of owning people as free labor teaches the true meaning of sweat equity, patient capital, and capitalism. African-Americans' first entrance into the American business model was not as an agent but as capital, or goods. Their skills and know-how were used to build the colony into a global superpower. The labor of those first movers enabled the initial harvest that funded the start-up operations of the migrators, who then used the returns to fuel the engine required for America to break free of European rule.

We are all different types of servants in different types of situations, and each situation has its gold in the land. My grandmother said, "The only thing God is not making any more of is time and land, so steward both wisely." Wise stewardship is what action is all about when transitioning from a creator of wealth to a wealth creator for yourself. For anyone to become a master, they must also be a servant. This is true in all things. It is through giving that one prepares to receive. The understanding of business makes the giving and receiving equitable; allowing both parties to value the exchange in whatever currencies they desire. Slavery, of any kind, can remain a thing of the past if we could learn to exchange and operate based on talents in the field of dreams and opportunities, where everyone has a value that must be paid in some form of the five capitals along The NarrowRoad.

Why does this matter? The lesson is to look not to the left nor the right but acknowledge the independent pursuit within you, and wisely steward your time and talents. Recognize the mastery level of those who came before you. Shifting your perspective in this way will provide opportunity and reward you, for your time, as you focus on the business development of yourself and others. Sometimes you have to work different parts of your field to uncover your hidden treasure buried within.

Summary of the Talents and Servant Levels

- Talent one: cultural capital
- Talent two: intellectual capital
- Talent three: human capital (People create knowledge, new ideas, and new products, and they establish relationships that make processes truly work. Unfortunately, when people leave, they take their knowledge; including internal, external, formal, and informal relationships.)
- Talent four: social capital
- Talent five: spiritual capital
- First servant: pools all five talents into a system that grows value everywhere they journey
- Second servant: exchanges weaknesses (talent four) for strengths (talent three) and builds collaborations to obtain access to up to four talents (talent two and talent one)
- Third servant: does all the work initially with his third talent (human capital); is successful in the short term but struggles to deliver results when working alone

I have spoken with thousands of individuals, many of them clients. The patterns I observe never cease to amaze me. They are patterns that can be traced back to the Israelites wandering in the wilderness, patterns which have followed through to our more recent history. The most prevalent patterns can be seen in our parents and grandparents. I will share a couple of examples of the mistakes many of us are making due to the blind spots in our legacies. These are the simple mistakes that could be the difference between achieving second or third servant level, instead of mastery. Some of these brief overviews illustrate some patterns that may seem familiar to you.

Angela and Troy owned three businesses and multiple homes together but were often short on cash. They were young, newly married, and making moves to generate as much income as possible, yet couldn't understand why they still struggled. Their response to lack was to start more money-making efforts. After all, having multiple side hustles was strongly encouraged in their generation.

While working with them, I asked how far in the future they'd looked to determine their level of financial health. Were they building a legacy that would lead to wealth? When examining their timescale, they realized that while they were accumulating assets and owning businesses, they were emergent-minded and committed to now. They had not yet learned how to look beyond their income to find their legacy. Essentially, they were burying their talent in the quicksand of quick moves, done all by themselves, with the best of intentions, devoid of financial expertise and practical tools to measure their progress. They were in third servant territory and needed an exit plan immediately.

We created a now budget, and it revealed there was no thinking or planning around their cash flow (the inflows and outflows of money), so when money came in, money also went out just as quickly. To cover their cash-flow shortages, they turned to debt, further impacting their cash flow and eventually ruining their credit.

It's a problem when we don't understand who we are in relation to the flow of our money. Money is simply our time, human capital multiplied by an hourly or annual wage. Without this understanding, we lose sight of how to balance the needs of ourselves and others, and we're not able to react in ways that build, grow, and expand opportunities. When faced with financial challenges, the fastest way to get hustled is to be on the hustle, and not aware of one's most vulnerable currency, which is time. You must first value *all* you have to value, other people, and understand their connection to building your lifestyle and reality. Typically, the way we do one thing is also the way we do everything. This behavior maps what we value most, and leads to a greater understanding of our necessary style of exchange, otherwise known as asking for help.

After working with the couple to help them shift their perspective further down the road toward legacy, they were able to see that positive cash flow was required to elevate their standard of business beyond that of survival. They promptly sold one of their properties, paid off some debt, started to save seriously, and managed their spending to a level within their means with the sound advice of a financial advisor. Once the picture they were posing for was framed, they were able to change their pose accordingly.

Perception versus Reality

Stacy ran her own business for nearly fifteen years. She was well-known, liked, respected and yet, barely making it. On the outside, she looked like a mover and shaker; receiving many awards for the impact she made in her community. But on the inside, she struggled to make ends meet and was bitterly aware of the contradiction between perception and reality. She came up to me after a speaking engagement and said, "I need to talk to you. I make too much money not to have any." Stacy was living a second servant life without the benefit of first servant models from which to learn. As a result, her success scared her, and she constantly felt at risk of losing it all quickly.

She needed financing to sustain and expand to a competitive scale. However, her accounting books were suspicious because she used her company as an ATM, so no bank would lend to her. She had tried and failed to find a partner to secure the added resources. She'd been going it alone for so long that she couldn't concede anything, making it nearly impossible to partner, co-build, or align with anyone.

On the surface, Stacy was a successful small businesswoman. She was resourceful, passionate, committed, capable, but inside, she was stuck because her understanding of money and her relationship with it was limited. But there was more to it than that. Because she was so financially illiterate, she was always insecure, and at a loss when money was involved and terrified of being hustled. That mistrust of herself translated into mis-trusting others and ultimately made her unable to pick the right partners, and make good deals. Stacey's fear made her unaware of what she did not know and almost impossible to teach alter-native ways to navigate further down the road to wealth.

What lies beneath the surface was how I was able to engage her with compassion. Her financial and business illiteracy was partnered with a level of financial oppression that spanned for generations. She felt shame that she had squandered her inheri-tance from both sides of the family, trying to look the part she had no clue how to master. While she grew up in a grower fam-ily, attended the right schools, and made the right connections, she had no clue how to expand it to the next level. She did know what it looked like, so the surface of appearances continued.

We worked together on growing her understanding of money so that she could interact with others from a place of confidence. I believe we were able to connect because all I wanted for Stacy was for her to exit her own financial wilderness. She learned how to identify and then face her fears, which unlocked her voice to ask for the help she needed to continue her journey to her promise. Stacy is now cash-flow positive and growing quite nicely. She enjoys having, and working with her team and with her banker, who wants her to succeed as much as she does.

It's Personal When It Should Be Business

He was an established pastor who came from a long line of ministers. He grew up in a home that was nothing like the one he'd created with his ministry. Which, at the time, served thousands of members. People traveled far and wide to attend his church. He had the heart of a father who wanted what he did not have growing up for those who attended his church. The congregation looked to him for guidance and support in everything, including finances. He desired to provide the support they needed as a ministry within the church. Yet financial, business literacy, and knowledge of how to raise the capital to build this area of ministry, did not presently live within the church leadership or congregation. Together, they wandered in the wilderness, looking for someone to unearth their treasure.

The support they needed required a different level of business acumen than the pastor and his leadership could provide. It required changes in the core of how they operated, namely working with a shared vision that lived outside the church's day-to-day operations and ministry. This had to include the financial regulations of systems in society, namely banking and insurance.

It was clear that financial and business acumen was needed to support such a dream. The pastor was often approached by people desiring to be of service to him and his congregation. Not quite confident himself of the fundamentals of personal finance, home and business ownership, he was not in a position to screen those who wanted to support his dream of assisting his congregation. He had not the *eyes* to protect both his own and his congregational vulnerabilities. He had the right intentions but the wrong level of emotional maturity to admit he was navigating uncharted territory outside of his degree of freedom.

The company that was brought in to advise the congregation was a small business with hidden agendas. The pastor was not able to recognize these hidden elements. As a result, many of the members walking in blind faith were either ill-advised or lost their homes and most of their retirement savings by investing in opportunities that were not in their best interest. Sadly, talents buried in the sand were taken away due to misinformation, miseducation and fear of going to people with a track record of advising clients; namely local and national banks in the area.

When I met this pastor, he was ashamed and depressed that his good intention could have gone so wrong. My belief is that when navigating uncharted territory, we need an expert who is adept, proven, and regulated; a master at the craft of which we are unsure. Our personal relationships with what could be well-intentioned but emergent businesses are not the way to lead those vulnerable to wealth creation. After building trust with this Pastor and his leadership, my first step was helping the pastor see that his first step on the long road to healing broken relationships, and devastated believers desiring to arrive at their Promised Land, was to separate the personal and the business. His relationship with money could no longer impact the church's desire to build a definition of wealth that could be taught and transferred across generations.

Lessons Learned Along The NarrowRoad

The following will help you better understand The NarrowRoad you are traveling. Answer as honestly as you can. If you're honest with yourself, your road will narrow to a path conducive to your success. There are no right or wrong answers, even if they don't match everything you've read in this book—remember, for legacy wealth to be attainable, it must be defined by you and the choices you understand.

There are three servant wealth builders. Which one are you?

1. You have proximity to masters of wealth creation who are willing to invest in you. You are aware of your 5 talents and are unafraid to multiply. If this is you, congratulations, you are a first servant.
2. You have proximity to successful leaders. You know the importance of a social network and how to use what you do best. You are unafraid to use your access to build wealth your way.
3. You have income, time, and proximity to others who are building lives they enjoy. You work hard; however, without supervision or a direct order to move or finish something, you prefer to play it safe, not wanting to lose what you have already gained.

Which of the following is your immediate desired outcome?

☐ Create a life with increased income—3rd servant lessons are most beneficial to you. Finish what you start and take the risks necessary to create what you need with what is within you. Manage your time well, and don't bury the opportunities given to you for safekeeping. They will expire and be taken from you. Your time is now. Use your 3rd quadrant to create the momentum you need to elevate your standard of wealth to a position of positive cash flow and comfort.

☐ Build a lifestyle you can sustain—2nd servant lessons are most beneficial to you. Budget for more than the moment, learn to give your best and receive what you need. Practice asking and advocating for yourself. Face your financial truth with a budget and a plan to own something that appreciates.

☐ Grow financially independent—1st servant lessons are most beneficial to you. Remain aware of your surroundings focus on ways to expand your territory. Invest in outcomes you desire that are further down the road. Model what you observe and admire.

☐ Expand the legacy—the Master's lessons are most beneficial for you. Understand that you must sow in fields where others will reap the harvests and recognize talent everywhere you go. Take chances on those who remind you of the stages along your wealth journey and invest where they need it most.

A hustle is when you are doing the work of vision, thought, action, speech, and achievement of outcomes all by yourself. The burden of this work is not easy; you are essentially choosing to shove your way down the road by any means necessary. This creates a storm of activity but very little long-term sustainable progress. The Master chose servants who could not do everything on their own.

They, in one way or another, needed investment to succeed at doing more with the gifts they possessed within themselves.

- Where are you on the hustle in your life journey? Is it your health, career, relationships, financial well-being or something else?
- What is driving your pursuit of wealth? Is it the perceptions of others or your lived and earned reality?
- Consider your degree of financial freedom desired. Is it externally or internally motivated? Who is defining your success?
- How does your personal relationship with money impact the business pursuits of your life? What if anything must you do differently to earn your 100% return on the talents you have been given?

Chapter Fifteen

WHY WE CAN'T WAIT

There is nothing new under the sun. The race is not to the swift, nor the battle to the strong, neither yet bread to the wise, nor yet riches to men of understanding, nor yet favor to women of skill; but time and chance happen to them all.

— Ecclesiastes 9:11(KJV)

After entering The NarrowRoad, you were given a roadmap that offered a step-by-step process to chart a path to reach your desired outcome. You learned that Strategy and Structure are your partners for wealth creation your way. The first objective of The NarrowRoad was to co-create a life business system to get you where you desire most to go—beyond the financial wilderness.

We've proven that we (as a nation) are wealth-builders. The battle becomes, how do you pick up the torch of that legacy for yourself? How do you make it your reality?

I once read a study that said 4 percent of us are leaders and 96 percent are followers. If that is true, you need to either pick up the torch and lead others in your community toward legacy wealth or follow someone holding the torch in front of you. One of these options is necessary for all to get to the Promised Land together. My grandfather said to me, "In life, there are always going to be many options, but there really is only one choice that is right for you, so choose wisely." Please follow the sage advice of Alphonse Jolly, Sr. It worked for him, and it can work for you as it has for me.

The title of this chapter is to ask another question that may inform a response to Dr. King's question. His book, *Why We Can't Wait* was his way to share the aims and goals of the civil rights movement to a larger audience who felt patience was the way forward when it came to integration and desegregation. The Civil Rights movement yielded many quantum leaps such as the Fair Housing Act, which ended redlining as a federal policy. Freedom comes in degrees that must be chosen as pursuits along the road to wealth your way. Today, we live in a world where the roadblocks our ancestors faced, and subsequently asked to wait for change, have been addressed. So, why are we waiting now? What is in the way for wealth to become a standard in our communities? I found specific reasons why we are waiting to build wealth our way. This chapter highlights a few of these roadblocks, in the hopes that you can navigate your way beyond them to the legacy wealth you desire.

Stuckpoint 1: Legacy Wealth Is Business and Personal

Wealth is not self-perpetuating. It does not build, grow, and expand on its own. Wealth requires a vision, a strategy, consistent action, relationships, and defined outcomes, to materialize into the value that matches the desires of the heart that is doing the building. It is for these reasons wealth manifests within a group process. A relationship first with your complete self (your history and legacy). Then with your ability to create resources from the talents you possess (your pursuit, roadmap, and journey). Then with your chosen community (marco view, the business of you). Finally, with your desired standard of living in this world (marco view, the business of you). The tighter and more connected the relationships, the fuller the life, and more realized the purpose, the deeper the faith, and greater the value of the wealth.

Creating wealth is simple, but it is not easy. Along the road to wealth creation are blind spots, that lead to rocky paths, that stem from missed and skipped steps necessary to mitigate risks everyone encounters when pursuing desires of their hearts. Risks are real, but the fear of them is a distraction from what you desire most in life; to realize all you are with all you have. Sometimes fear keeps us safe, but sometimes it holds us back. Understanding your relationship with risk is knowing the difference.

The need to mitigate risk is how your choices narrow the road to wealth amid many options. This is your life journey, and to get what you want, you must understand how to best protect and grow what you have. This is accomplished when you clarify your vision of what wealth will enable you to do in your everyday life. The level of risk you are willing to take is up to you; the level of wealth you will build is up to your choices about managing the risks along your NarrowRoad to legacy wealth.

Wealth requires you to attach to desired outcomes located further down the road, beyond what is readily seen. What is it that you desire for your life, your family, your community? What is your role in bringing about these outcomes? Where must others assist? A large part of legacy wealth is the convergence of your faith and finances. You have to believe in your ability to create wealth for yourself however you define it, and that belief invites others to join you. An agreement can mitigate risks. Agreements require communication with others about your desires and the fears attached to pursuing them. The further you go down the road, the more you will find yourself charting a path along a narrower road that is often less traveled. The increased usage of big data and machine learning tools is becoming mainstream. I still contend that a culturally relevant tool for African-Americans, such as The NarrowRoad Identity, is still a rarity in the world in which we live. For too long, wealth was something hidden in the field of affluence and the upwardly mobile. But everyone, in their way, wants to get there. Products and services for the affluent are more accessible, but the means and modes of producing a sustainable journey to wealth, while enjoying them, are still hidden in plain sight. Now is the time for you to stretch your ability to believe you can live a life you desire, including saving, investing, and transferring wealth to the next generation. We can all get out of the financial wilderness and onto a road to wealth our way. This book has given you the steps, so why are you waiting?

Stuckpoint 2: The Way You Begin Is Not the Way You End

The journey toward wealth is in its genesis, and individual pursuit, with a series of glimpses created exclusively for your personal development. The first glimpse is one given to you through the lens of your legacy (Quadrant 1). The second glimpse is what begins your learning journey, unlocking your genius code to pursue opportunities unique to you (Quadrant 2). The third glimpse is what creates your mission with the talents you currently have in your possession, to earn the income to build the seeds of your wealth (Quadrant 3). The fourth glimpse begins the collective movement forward, by exchanging your strengths for assistance with navigating the roadmap, to the desires of your heart (Quadrant 4).

Your pursuit of wealth, as you define it, is your business. That business engages and exchanges with collective processes such as education, community, voting, crowd-funding, and equity investing. Staying focused on your pursuit by leveraging your personal systems for success while remaining aware of the necessary collective processes is how you navigate further down the road.

Everyone has a genesis and an exodus in their lives. Your genesis is the starting point of your journey. Your introduction to business began with your childhood—the family business. How your family managed the household operations, and your role in it, is the genesis of your life pursuit.

- So how did your family manage money?
- What did your childhood teach you to do, and not to do, with money?
- Which statement best describes your experience within this phase of development?
- What do you want to do differently?
- Where have you shifted your perspective to make those changes?
- What questions do you still have to ask to increase your confidence level in making these desired changes and mitigate risk?
- What must you do now to take that next step?

- What can't you do alone?
- Who must you ask for help?

You must answer these questions for yourself to build upon your genesis and get beyond the wilderness onto your Narrow-Road. Your answers have been explored throughout this book. Should you desire a wealth group to assist you in answering them and holding you accountable, extend your journey along The NarrowRoad to www.mynarrowroad.com/wealthgroup.

By now, you know The NarrowRoad journey through the wilderness leads to a custom-designed path toward legacy wealth. It is customized because it is based on your own choices and definition of wealth. It is meant to be stress-free, exciting, and filled with learning opportunities. Getting through the wilderness is owning your choices with your NarrowRoad identity. You do this by ordering your steps to get to where you most desire to go. With your NRID, you now have this tool to build your system for success.

Your Wealth Journey Is Dimensional

What may not be clear is that The NarrowRoad has dimensions. Dimensions are aspects and inflection points. Each dimension further clarifies how you define wealth and what you desire it to be in your life.

To remove the obstacles blocking your legacy wealth perspective, look first at what you can afford to model differently for your family legacy, then explore how to best face whatever challenges appear before you and move on from there. This is your contribution to the legacy of your family business. It matters that you succeed in pursuing what you see as most important to continue the legacy forward to wealth as you've defined. Align yourself with your legacy perspective, and you are on your way.

To pursue your dream of financial independence, organize (your power) people and money; prioritize what is important. Your partnership is with the priorities in your life and getting you and them beyond the financial wilderness.

To get out of the storm of doing all things independently, and to act on your true mission, operate your business as a talent multiplier both intrapreneurial and entrepreneurially.

To build the life you want, speak your truth about wealth with those you trust and want to get there with you. Your share of the wealth enterprise involves a group.

To ensure you stay on your NarrowRoad, connect with a goal you consider important to reach. How far can you afford to look down the road now? What outcomes motivate you?

So Where Are You in the Wilderness?

You own your position in the wilderness with the answers to the following question: Why have I not gone beyond my present financial situation? Is it a lack of order or a lack of structure? A lack of faith, or not facing my financial truth?

For wealth to be real, you must believe it is possible for you on your terms, with your unique variables that create your wealth equation. Your wealth equation is how you define wealth on your terms. Lack of definition leads to a lack of direction. That leads to the crowd who are journeying through the wide-open gate, only to find themselves wandering in the financial wilderness with all of their good intentions.

Wealth requires more than good intentions. It demands that you pay attention to your vision, thoughts, actions, and speech. Wealth expects you to have desired outcomes. It is promised that once aligned, you will be given the desires of your heart, but you must define what they are, and how others can help you get there.

Seventeen years ago, I knew I wanted wealth to be something less complicated. I marveled at how those with audacious goals and determination did not always succeed at first, but they kept moving forward. They seemed to attract success by the way they desired it. When I attended my twentieth reunion at Hampton University (my beloved home by the sea), I realized I had not returned since my tenth reunion. My father loved to go every year. It reminded him of my journey, and how far I had come from a little girl hoping to become a woman pursuing dreams well-worn from both success and failure. As I walked the campus, I remembered my great-grandmother, who had come to visit me my sophomore year. I passed the place where my father loved to sit by the water that was close to where my mother enjoyed walking by the sailboats. I realized then that Hampton represented a part of my legacy wealth promise. One of the few Historically Black Colleges that has had the same president for generations, Hampton represents a vision that took time to mold, fund, support, and expand. I was able to see what was not so readily apparent twenty-four years ago, when I began my contribution to the Hampton legacy. While the seeds were planted with me, it took twenty additional graduating classes to reveal it in its entirety. Many things I cherished about my Hampton experience are gone. But what remains are the memories as I share them in my narrative, the relationships I cherish with those who experienced what I experienced, and the ability to continue to play a role in the expansion of the vision for another twenty years.

Working in the financial services industries in many roles with various responsibilities and perspectives, I have seen the evolution of legacy to wealth. Where there were laws, rules, and regulations that kept segments of our population from owning and building wealth, things are changing. The Joint Center for Housing at Harvard reported that by 2025 there would be seventeen million new homeowners, and 76 percent of these new homeowners will be from diverse markets. Homeownership is a major driver of wealth creation, and will become a standard in communities that three generations ago struggled with financing. The wheel continues to turn, and so must we with it.

Along The NarrowRoad, you will find that the patterns within these four roles (vision, thought, action, speech) reveal your legacy, strategy, mission, and purpose. Traveling The NarrowRoad will reveal your fears and the deepest desires of your heart. When you take the ordered steps and connect the dots of these simple elements, you will trust and believe in the promise that wealth is possible for you. Legacy wealth is self-perpetuating. Legacy wealth connects the dots from the past to the present to the future. It creates a three-corded strand, that is not easily broken once connected, and tied to a future that you often have to "believe to eventually see." This is how your faith and finance connect to build from the wealth hidden within you.

The NarrowRoad meets you where you are in the wealth-creation process and helps you chart a path to however far down the road you desire to go (legacy and its transfer). Hope is not the only thing that springs eternal. Wealth can spring forth eternal opportunities if you take the time to write the vision and make it plain so that generation after generation can run with it. Legacy wealth, in this light, is a system that ensures visions come to pass in their appointed time. No need to commit your life to hustle, when you've taken the time to write your legacy wealth blueprint that you can pass on.

We are the best teachers but the worst students of our lesson plans. Walk your talk and live up to your standard, things take time. Everything has a process. As my grandmother would often say, "The only thing God is not making any more of is time and land, so steward them appropriately."

Reviewing Why We Are Waiting to Build Legacy Wealth

The glimpse in Chapter 15 is that things take time. Everything has a process. The only thing God is not making any more of is time and land, so we must learn to steward resources unique to our lives and legacies appropriately. Legacy wealth is waiting for us to explore and develop it; believe this, and the wait is over.

If you wish to continue on The NarrowRoad, join the journey by visiting mynarrowroad.com and chart your path to legacy wealth today.

GLOSSARY OF TERMS

During my research, I asked thousands of people to define seven keywords. The process revealed that while we say the same words, we often do not mean the same things. As a result, a lot gets lost in translation when we talk about wealth, legacy and money. Along The NarrowRoad, you will come to own these definitions in your pursuit of legacy wealth.

Acumen—the ability to make shrewd and strategic decisions.

Capital—wealth in the form of money or other assets owned by a person or an organization.

Capital, cultural—your perspective based on the lived experiences of you, your family, and your community. Cultural capital is unique to you and your legacy. It is the lens through which you can see what others cannot initially see.

Capital, human—knowledge, skills, experiences, intuition, and attitudes used to earn income in the workforce.

Capital, intellectual—applied knowledge that is of value, useful for establishing partnerships to grow.

Capital, social—who you know, how you connect, and how you exchange value.

Capital, spiritual—what you believe, who you believe, why you believe, and how you affirm your faith in what you believe.

Capital exchanges—there are four capital exchanges along The NarrowRoad. Capital exchanges are how you exchange the five resources you have in your portfolio of talents.

Exchange 1: Sympathetic Capital—an exchange where you jump all in into another person's current situation to assist others.

Exchange 2: Empathetic Capital—an exchange where you partially enter into another person's current situation to assist others.

Exchange 3: Apathetic Capital—an exchange where you avoid situations that require you to assist others not on par with your standard of living.

Exchange 4: Compassionate Capital—an exchange where you invite others to consider the solution you have taken to address an issue or situation they are currently facing.

Entrepreneur—a person who organizes and operates a business or businesses, taking on greater than normal financial risks.

Financial Equity—the value of an ownership interest in property, including shareholder equity in a business. Equity or shareholders´ equity is part of the total capital of a business.

Financial Literacy—the ability to use knowledge and skills to manage one's financial resources effectively for lifetime financial security.

Financial Plan—a report that identifies a person's financial goals, needs, and expected future earning, saving, investing, insurance, and debt management activities. It typically includes a statement of net worth (equity) and an ongoing thinking process to develop an orderly program or blueprint for handling all aspects of one's money, including spending, credit, saving, and investing.

Intrapreneurship—the act of behaving like an entrepreneur while working within a large organization.

Legacy—a narrative that does not begin with you and will not end with you unless you remain stuck in your financial wilderness story.

Legacy Wealth—the convergence of one's faith in his or her future and the ongoing financial stewardship of past and present resources. Legacy wealth is used to successfully navigate out of the financial wilderness and onto a path toward promise.

Margin of Safety—a metric used to better understand the impact of change or loss of income on your current financial situation.

NRID—your NarrowRoad ID, a code that once applied to your life, reveals your system of success path toward legacy wealth.

NREQ—The NarrowRoad Equation, a string of variables that, when pursued in sequence, results in possession of a desired outcome.

Personal finance—the principles and methods individuals use to acquire and manage income and assets.

Quantum Leap—a carefully executed path beyond the financial wilderness using your NRID in the four terrains (rocky, thorny, fertile, landmines).

Value system—a set of criteria, standards, or principles that guide an individual or group's behavior and provide a sense of direction to life.

Values, cultural—prevailing beliefs and value systems of a given society passed on through social conditioning/enculturation.

Values, individual—an individual's beliefs about what is important, desirable, and worthwhile, which often influences decisions.

Vision, financial—a description of how an individual defines future financial success and what they want to accomplish. It provides direction for decisions and actions that invent the preferred future. What will the future look like if financial strategies are successfully implemented, and one's full potential is achieved?

Wealth-building—increasing the total value of what one owns. One's tangible assets using strategies to increase savings and personal asset accumulation, thereby promoting individual/family economic well-being and financial security.

Wealth-creator—a person on The NarrowRoad who is committed to creating, building, growing, and expanding legacy wealth for themselves and generations to come.

APPENDIX

What is an accredited investor? Usually, they are sophisticated investors who are financially savvy. In the United States, an accredited investor is someone who meets the requirements established by the Securities and Exchange Commission to participate in large-scale investment transactions. Individuals who are accredited investors meet at least one of the following criteria:

- Earn an individual annual income of more than $200,000 or a joint annual income of $300,000 for the last two years and have the reasonable expectation of maintaining the same income level for the current year.
- Have a net worth exceeding $1 million, either individually or jointly with their spouse.
- Serve as a general partner, executive officer, director, or similar role for the issuer of a security being offered.

For more information, please visit the Securities and Exchange Commission site.

What Is a Non-Accredited Investor? A non-accredited investor simply does not meet the Securities and Exchange Commission requirements to become an accredited investor.

Proposed Rules: Consistent with the JOBS Act, the proposed rules would, among other things, permit individuals to invest, subject to certain thresholds, limit the amount of money a company can raise, require companies to disclose certain information about their offers, and create a regulatory framework for the intermediaries that would facilitate the crowdfunding transactions.

Under the proposed rules:

- A company would be able to raise a maximum aggregate amount of $1 million through crowdfunding offerings in twelve months.

- Investors, for twelve months, would be permitted to invest up to:

- Two thousand dollars, or 5 percent of their annual income or net worth, whichever is greater, if both their annual income and net worth are less than $100,000.

- Ten percent of their annual income or net worth, whichever is greater, if either their annual income or net worth is equal to or more than $100,000. During the twelve months, these investors would not be able to purchase more than $100,000 of securities through crowd-funding.

  http://www.sec.gov/News/PressRelease/Detail/PressRelease/1370540017677#.U_oXel7tKll.

ACKNOWLEDGMENTS

Seventeen years was a long time to work towards and focus on one thing. Along the road, as it narrowed, countless people helped me in ways they may not even know. Not only do I thank you, but I also have and will continue to pray for you and your legacy wealth journey. I know that one day our paths will cross again, and I will return the favor you bestowed on my life just when I needed it most. I am living proof that if you want to go far, you must go together.

In the midst of the many (and I do mean many) who supported my journey as I narrowed my road, there are a few who I must mention:

The Investors—those visionaries who planted the financial seed into the journey and confirmed my path was for me: Bessie Pearl Horne (my grandmother), Sylvia Jolly (my mother), Vincent Jolly Sr. (my father, may he rest in peace), Vincent Jolly Jr. (my brother), Eulena B. Horne (my aunt), Avis Scott Schwartz (my cousin), Ophelia Foote (my great aunt), Jasmine Bellamy, Nichol Bradford, Miriam Torres, Tonia Spence, Dr. Marisa Rogers, Eston Griffin, Drs. Brenda and James Rogers, Arthur Roland, Asantewaa Phoenix, Tina Eskridge, Linwood and Kathi Jolly, Rev. William (Billy) Jolly (my cousin), Bill Jolly (my cousin), Mark Randall, Wilmont Allen, Joyce Ntim, & Bishop Leon J. Petty (rest in peace).

The Strategists—those thinkers whose expertise helped me gain confidence in believing in and building The Narrow-Road: Stanley Tucker, Bennie L. Horne Jr. (my uncle), Charles Harris, Marcus Adams, Robert Barrimond, Carla Harris, Kathia and Shane Dennis, Dr. Cheryl Miller, Kizzie Bozeman, Glen Boykin, Barthaniel Werts, Michael Rapelyea, Christopher Nazzereth, Mark Randall, Joy Jordan, Lesley Steward, Rod Stanley, Dr. Peter Paris, Dr. Charles Adams, Dr. Shawn Copeland, Jacob Cobb Mays III, Nigel Henry, Terrence Damon Barclift, Trevor Ott, Che Brown, & Charles Wooding.

The Builders—Those doers whose engagements with Torch Enterprises allowed me to perfect The NarrowRoad curricula and workshop materials: My Pastor clients, The fast girls, Alpha Phi Alpha Fraternity, Inc., Alpha Kappa Alpha Sorority, Inc., NAREB, UNCF, 1st District AME, Enon Tabernacle Baptist Church, Mocha Mom's, RIISE, Tabernacle International Deliverance Church, The Empowerment Network, Russell Technology Business Incubator and countless entrepreneurs and their communities.

The Connectors—those speakers who helped me build The NarrowRoad system by opening their mouths and spreading the word of my desire to elevate the standard of legacy to wealth in our communities: Rev. Charisse Tucker, Dr. George Fraser, Georgette Dixon, Cheryl McDonald, Brenda Wright, Greg Young, Marva Allen, Cerita Battle, Beverly Ferguson, C. Renee Wilson, Mandala Jones, Doris Canty-Brown, Anika Khan, Pastor Rossie Francis, Carlos and Winifred Bell, Lorisa Bates, Tonia Petty, Renee Carracter, Janice Hopkins, Keisha Chandler, Michele Lawrence, Laura Roane, William D. Lyle, Edgar Carter, Shawn Dove, Anthony Smith, Trabian Shorters.

The Deliverers of Outcomes—Those chance moments that gave me the encouragement to keep on going at the bends in the road of this journey: 100 Black Men National Conferences, Wells Fargo Legacy Wealth Events, Mocha Mom's National Conference, UNCF Legacy Wealth Breakfasts, NAACP Leadership Summit, Urban League National Conference, Thurgood Marshall

Foundation Youth Conference, Bethune Cookman University's Woman's Conference, Wharton African-American Alumni Network, NAREB SHIBA Events, NAREB National Conferences, George Fraser's PowerNetworking Conferences, the Omaha Legacy Wealth Initiative Cohort, The Family Business Cohort, The Women and Wealth Cohort (Philadelphia), The Black Male Equity Initiative Cohort (Detroit).

CPSIA information can be obtained
at www.ICGtesting.com
Printed in the USA
BVHW050251100522
636492BV00007B/17/J